Studebaker

THE COMPLETE HISTORY

Patrick Foster

CRESTLINE

*This book is dedicated to those proud
keepers of the flame—my fellow members of
the Studebaker Drivers Club.*

Library of Congress Cataloging-in-Publication Data

Foster, Patrick R.
  Studebaker / Patrick Foster.
    p. cm.
  Includes bibliographical references and index.
  ISBN 978-0-7858-3261-4
  1. Studebaker automobile—History. I. Title.
  TL215.S79F67 2008
  338.7'629220973--dc22

                                    2008009018

On the cover: 1955 Studebaker President.

On the frontispiece: 1938 President Coupe.

On the title pages: 1957 Golden Hawk. *Mike Mueller*

On the contents page: 1954 Commander Starlight V-8 Coupe.

On the back cover, main: 1963 Avanti. *Mike Mueller*
Inset: 1956 President station wagon

Editor: Chris Endres
Designer: Jennie Maas

Printed in China

Table of Contents

Acknowledgments

The author wished to express his thanks to Paul Brothers, Buell Martin, John Katz, Bill Wilson, Amy Christman, and Mike Mueller. Special thanks go to my editor Chris Endres, who was able to put up with my tantrums and keep the book moving ahead, and to my publisher Zack Miller for giving me the opportunity to create the sort of book I feel the hobby deserves.

Introduction

Studebaker was once numbered among the largest companies in America, staffed with bright young men of great drive and skill. They produced huge numbers of vehicles; great cars and trucks made with high-quality materials, sold through a network of experienced dealers, and backed by excellent service.

And yet they failed.

There's a lesson to be learned from that. In this era of intense competition in the auto industry, of Japanese product onslaughts, an invasion of low-priced Chinese cars, unequal market access for American products, damaged brands, and a mountain of legacy costs facing America's automakers, the story of Studebaker's rise and fall has far more relevance than all the tired advice and outlandish warnings spouted by an army of self-important analysts.

The meltdown of the grand old Studebaker company was astounding to witness. The span of time between its joyous 100th anniversary celebration, when it was one of the most successful automobile companies in the world, and the closing of the main plant in South Bend, Indiana, was a mere eleven years—and would have occurred years earlier if not a for a last-minute bailout. When Studebaker's Canadian plant closed down a little over two years later the company was completely and permanently out of the car business. Considering its onetime position as the largest vehicle producer in the world, it was a downfall almost without precedence. And yet out of that devastating loss a new company emerged, bearing the name of the old one, but smaller, leaner, and more diverse, a configuration that would become known as a mini-conglomerate.

Herein lies the story of one of America's great transportation giants, a proud company that supplied vehicles to the Union Army during the Civil War and went on to build vehicles for World War One, World War Two, the Korean Conflict, and Vietnam. With roots reaching back to well before the automobile was first conceived, Studebaker still holds the record as the longest-standing transportation company in America.

I'll leave it to the reader to decide whether the greater lesson to be learned herein stems from Studebaker's spectacular fall from grace or from its equally dramatic rebirth. But automotive executives everywhere should be cautioned to guard against complacency. History has illustrated time and again that such an approach can lead to ruin.

Patrick R. Foster

July 4, 2008

This woodcarving from the 1952 Studebaker *Centennial Report* depicts the company's humble beginnings as a blacksmith shop. "From tiny acorns do Great Oaks spring!"

CHAPTER ONE

1852-1902
An Inspired Heritage

The Lincoln automobile is named for one of America's greatest presidents. Yet the vehicle Abraham Lincoln used for conveyance was a Studebaker. Legend has it that in the 1850s a struggling farmer named Ulysses Grant often drove a Studebaker wagon loaded with firewood to town, earning a bare living and hoping his luck would change. A few years later, Studebaker wagons would transport thousands of tons of supplies for his mighty armies in the campaigns of the American Civil War. Years after the close of his career as America's greatest general, President Grant rode in public in a Studebaker carriage, a vehicle that was like the man himself: sturdy, honest, and unpretentious.

For many years, Studebaker held the proud claim as the vehicle owned by more Americans than any other brand. No mere local or regional phenomenon, Studebaker vehicles were known and respected around the world. An argument could be made that Studebaker was the first truly global vehicle brand. Studebaker was the natural choice of princes, kings, and presidents.

More important than the exalted dignitaries were the tens of thousands of ordinary citizens who purchased Studebaker wagons for use in their daily work. After all, Studebaker produced every kind of horse-drawn vehicle imaginable, including two-wheel carts, farm wagons, freight wagons, road sprinklers, paddy wagons, light delivery wagons, and heavy mining wagons that could haul two tons. In addition to work vehicles, Studebaker produced just about every other kind, from simple buggies and bobsleds to elegant carriages. Each of them was built with the care and skill that became a Studebaker trademark. There were even Studebakers for children: fun little carts designed to be pulled by a dog or a goat.

Today, millions of Americans still recall the glorious years when Studebaker manufactured a broad range of trucks, military vehicles, and some of the best-looking automobiles ever to grace the American road.

Studebaker was one of America's first great manufacturing enterprises. The company had always focused on transportation. Long before there was a Studebaker car there was a Studebaker wagon, and it served the country's needs like no other vehicle had. Decades before the automobile industry was born, Studebaker boasted being the largest vehicle producer in the world. And the world took notice.

In an age when American industry was beginning to blossom on the world's stage, Studebaker was viewed as an economic dynamo, with an amazing capacity for production. Studebaker and its vehicles reflected the beliefs of the men whose name they bore. The Studebakers who

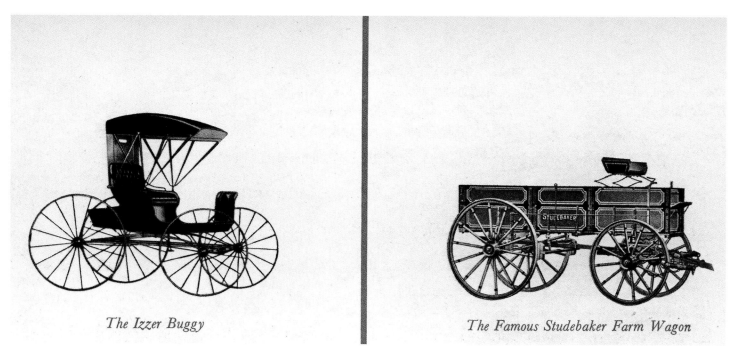

The Izzer Buggy

The Famous Studebaker Farm Wagon

At left we see the famous Studebaker Izzer Buggy, and to the right is a Studebaker Farm Wagon.

The Studebaker brothers, from left: Clement, Henry, Jacob, Peter, and J. M. (John Mohler, also known as "Wheelbarrow Johnny").

The Studebaker Brothers' Ashland, Ohio, blacksmith shop.

Although John Studebaker had gained a measure of success he was, like many Americans of that era, restless to strike out for new lands and new opportunities. He decided to join the great westward movement, resolving to move his family and himself to fresh new country. Around 1835 he built a sturdy Conestoga-type wagon pulled by four horses. In this simple device John Studebaker, his wife, Rebecca Mohler, whom he'd married in 1820, and their six children made the journey to the rugged land out west. They took with them two other wagons loaded with tools, utensils,

founded the company in 1852 were hardy men of trade, men who had come up by the sweat of their brows. Yet as enormous as it became, the giant enterprise began as a simple blacksmith shop in what was then the distant West by two brothers named Studebaker.

The Studebakers believed in hard work, thrift, and kindness to their fellow man. Their ancestors, Peter, Clement, Henry, Anna Margetha, and Anna Catherine Studebaker, arrived in America on September 1, 1736. They had sailed from Rotterdam, Holland, on the ship *Harle*, landing in Philadelphia. Strong men of good German stock, blacksmithing would be a family tradition. Peter Studebaker settled in what was then Huntingdon Township in York County, Pennsylvania, eventually establishing a blacksmith and woodwork shop with his son, Peter Jr.

In time, Peter Jr. married and had a son named John, who in turn became the father of the young men who would found the Studebaker Company. John Studebaker lived in Adams County, Pennsylvania, near Gettysburg, where he built a brick house and blacksmith shop. In addition to his skill as a smithy, he also earned a reputation as a skilled wagon builder.

and an anvil so John could practice his trade when they arrived at their destination. Back then, America did not stretch uninterrupted from sea to shining sea. What folks called the West is what today we call the Midwest: Ohio, Michigan, and Indiana. The Studebakers settled in Ashland, Ohio, where John built a home and a blacksmith shop. Over the door he hung a handmade sign, a personal motto reflecting his simple faith, burned into a wood plank. It read: *"Owe No Man Anything but to Love One Another."*

Although things looked promising at first, the economy eventually went bad, and John Studebaker experienced financial difficulties. By 1850, John and Rebecca decided once again to move their family: sons Henry, Clement, John Mohler, Peter, and Jacob, and daughter Maria. They moved farther west, to South Bend, Indiana, an attractive little town on the St. Joseph River.

By 1851, the family was settled in South Bend, and the following year two of the boys decided to go into business for themselves. On February 16, 1852, Henry and Clement established a new business they called H&C Studebaker. The company engaged in blacksmithing, woodworking, and

The company began in 1852, and this illustration shows the farm wagon it produced. Only a small number of these were built in the early years, but in time Studebaker would become the largest wagon producer in the country.

building wagons to order. From this humble beginning the tiny firm would eventually grow to become one of the largest companies in the nation. The old saying that from tiny acorns spring forth mighty oaks is well displayed herein; the total start-up capital of H&C Studebaker was a mere $68. The shop's assets included two forges, hand tools, and the combined skill and determination of two young men.

On their first day in business, they had just one customer, a local man named Harper who had two shoes changed on his horse. From that modest start, work picked up slowly but steadily. Later in that first year, George Earl hired them to build a farm wagon. It took them seven days to build it; they painted it green and red with the name *Studebaker* in big yellow letters. Their bill: $175 complete. It was the first of millions of vehicles that would bear the Studebaker name. But the wagon business didn't immediately take off after that hopeful start. It would be years before the brothers would be able to abandon the blacksmithing trade and become full-time vehicle builders.

Meanwhile, in early 1853, Clem and Henry's younger brother John Mohler Studebaker, just 19 years old, decided to strike out on his own

in the world. Ever since gold had been discovered at Sutter's Mill, young men from around the country had pulled up stakes and begun the long trek to the furthermost lands, hoping to strike it rich in the California gold fields. John Mohler found a wagon train that would take him there in exchange for a new Studebaker wagon. His brothers built a sturdy wagon, his mother sewed $65 into his belt and packed him a Bible and three suits of clothes, and he set off to make his way in the world.

The vast expanse of country between home and California was a dry, thirsty land teeming with desperados, rough cowboys, and pitiless Indians. It took over five months of hard traveling to make it from Ohio to the small mining town of Old Dry Diggens, home to some 2,000 souls. This was truly the Wild West. To enforce the law the town had hanged so many men that the place became known as Hangtown.

When John Mohler arrived there in August 1853, a crowd of curious folk gathered around the newcomers asking for news of the world outside. A man named Joe Hinds called out asking if anyone was a wagon maker, and young John Mohler answered back that he was. Hinds offered him a

The Studebaker Brothers shop and offices in South Bend, Indiana.

This postcard shows the Centennial Wagon that was displayed at Philadelphia's Centennial Exposition in 1876. The bottom picture shows the Studebaker wagon displayed at Chicago's Columbian Exposition in 1893. The postcard isn't dated but may have been produced for Studebaker's 100th anniversary.

job making wheelbarrows, but the youngster, his head filled with thoughts of gold nuggets, declined saying he'd come to California to dig for gold and that was what he aimed to do. As Hinds walked away a kindly stranger offered John Mohler some sound advice. "Young man," he said, "take that job and take it quick!" adding that there would be plenty of time to dig for gold, but good jobs were scarce. What had been offered was a mighty good opportunity. Though John Mohler was not yet 20, he saw the wisdom of the advice, caught up with Hinds, and took the job.

John Mohler made wheelbarrows, shod horses, and fixed wagons and stagecoaches. He stayed in Hangtown five years, saving his money. By 1856, the town changed its name to Placerville. John Mohler continued to stay in touch with his family by mail, receiving regular letters from his brothers.

H&C Studebaker was still in business and by that time was producing a dozen or so wagons a year, but still doing a lot of blacksmithing. They had gotten a taste of producing vehicles in large volume when the Mishawaka Wagon Works subcontracted with them to build 100 army wagons to help fill a large order. Suddenly needing large amounts of seasoned lumber, the Studebakers devised a kiln that could dry green timbers quickly, then hired men to help them produce the wagons in half the time for which the contract called.

It was an epiphany of sorts; the realization that if they could somehow get sufficient orders, they could build more wagons than was ever thought possible. Volume production would reduce costs, allowing lower prices that would spur demand. But of course, in order to begin volume production they would need to buy large amounts of materials with which to build the wagons, and that took lots of money. All the brothers needed to expand the business, they realized, was an influx of working capital.

Out in California, "Wheelbarrow Johnny" Mohler had saved up some $8,000. After reading his brothers' letters explaining how much they felt they could expand the business if only they had some additional capital, John Mohler came home to South Bend in June 1858 with the idea of investing his money in H&C Studebaker to fund expanded wagon production. His brother Henry, however, wasn't interested in growing the business; he longed for the quiet life of a farmer. John Mohler bought out Henry's share of the business, staking his capital on the future of H&C Studebaker.

By 1860, the Studebakers were producing a wide range of wheeled transportation. They convinced their youngest brother, Peter, to offer their wagons in his general store in Goshen, Indiana, in the process creating their first out-of-town showroom. A new shed is really all it was, but it represented the first of many Studebaker dealerships that were to follow. The Studebakers had more than a dozen men on the payroll, and their products were sold throughout Indiana. Then the Civil War came, and the brothers received contracts to build thousands of wagons for the Union Army. They had to continually expand to keep up with demand.

STUDEBAKER CARRIAGE MANUFACTORY, SOUTH BEND, INDIANA

This circa 1874 illustration of the Studebaker wagon works gives some idea of how large the company had grown. Good products at a fair price were the ingredients that created Studebaker's success.

mainly by wagon, many of them made by Studebaker because the brand was known by ex-soldiers everywhere as a wagon they could trust. Before long, Studebaker sales outlets were established in hundreds of towns across the land. With the advent of the Transcontinental Railroad, the company began shipping finished wagons by rail to the rapidly expanding West.

By 1867, they were producing 6,000 vehicles a year, and it was time to put things on a more professional basis reflecting the company's larger size. On March 26, 1868, the business was incorporated as the Studebaker Brothers Manufacturing Company. Peter Studebaker joined the firm and was put in charge of sales and marketing. Clement was in charge of production. To formalize their roles, Peter and Clem signed an agreement that read:

The end of the war didn't mean the end of expansion. When hostilities ended, war-weary soldiers began to move en masse to the West, establishing farms, building homesteads, growing the nation. They moved

I, Peter Studebaker, agree to sell all the wagons my brother Clem can make.
(Signed) Peter Studebaker
I agree to make all he can sell.
(Signed) Clem Studebaker

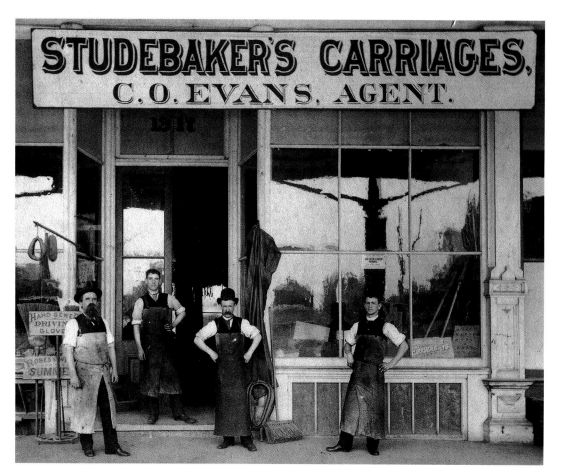

There's no recorded explanation why John Mohler Studebaker didn't sign any sort of promise, but as the man who had brought the company into the big time and who labored continually to grow the business, perhaps they felt it wasn't necessary to secure his pledge. A couple of years later, their brother Jacob joined the firm. The Studebaker men, all

C. O. Evans was an agent for Studebaker. Agents later became known as dealers. Studebaker had a vast network of agents selling its products. Many of these would form the nucleus of the automotive dealer network.

A fine-looking horse and a handsome buggy were a perfect match for a ride in the country.

as full-bearded as the Smith Brothers, were building a family-run company that would eventually outgrow the ability of one family to run it.

There were occasional setbacks. Fires in 1872 and 1874 burned down several buildings and wiped out stocks of raw materials. But the brothers soon rebuilt, and each time they did, the buildings were larger than before. By now there was scarcely a person in America unfamiliar with their products.

In 1885, Jacob Studebaker died at the young age of 43. His brother Peter was the next to go, passing on in 1897, just days after the company celebrated its 45th year in business. By that point, the company's annual sales were more than $2.5 million, and the firm had long since hired several younger professionals to help manage the business. One of these was Frederick Fish, a New Jersey corporate lawyer and son-in-law of John Mohler. After Peter's death, Fred Fish was named president of the Studebaker Brothers Manufacturing Company, and for the first time a Studebaker was not in charge of the business.

Frederick Fish was a great deal younger than the Studebakers, and young men tend to think boldly. Fish was aware that several inventors had produced carriages that moved without the aid of horses—*horseless carriages* was the term many people used to describe them—and he wanted Studebaker to consider that business. In 1896, a small sum was set aside to explore the possibility of producing an electric-powered carriage. Around 1897 or 1898, the company began to manufacture bodies for electric taxicabs produced by the Electric Vehicle Company. However, this was viewed mainly as a way to generate more work for the coach factory. During the next few years Studebaker reportedly looked into buying a vehicle firm, but nothing came of it.

Clement Studebaker died in 1901, leaving John Mohler (J. M.) Studebaker as the last brother to survive. J. M. was still a hale and hearty man, and although he initially considered the horseless carriage a passing fad, he didn't stand in the way when others in the firm wanted to become more active in that emerging business.

At Fish's instigation, the company finally introduced a line of Studebaker cars in 1902. They were conservative to say the least, modest runabouts powered by batteries and capable of reliable transportation. They were meant to be an adjunct to the core line of wagons, an interesting, albeit minor, addition to the existing business.

In 1902, America and the world still moved around primarily by horse-drawn wagons, carriages, and trolleys. The new vehicles had barely earned themselves a distinct name, since many people still called them horseless carriages, although the term *automobile* was coming more into use. Many people still said they were a fad, and the enthusiasm for them would soon die out. But the little Studebaker Electrics were part of the vanguard in the industry's relentless growth. From these would spring forth mighty cars and an even mightier company. Although neither Fish nor J. M. could know it, the firm they had devoted their lives to was about to experience growth that was greater than even the most delirious visionary could have foretold.

NO. 1354. STUDEBAKER RUNABOUT
STICK SEAT. NO TOP

Studebaker's entry into the automobile business began in 1902 with the introduction of a line of electric-powered vehicles. These drew heavily on the company's long experience building carriages. These so-called horseless carriages were simple machines. Shown here is the No. 1354 Runabout, a basic vehicle with a "stick seat and no top," according to the brochure.

CHAPTER TWO

1902-1933

Emergence of a Great Automobile Company

The new Studebaker cars debuted in 1902. Offered in electric-powered models only, they were not, strictly speaking, brilliant automobiles; but they demonstrated sound engineering and, like all Studebaker's at that time, were built with good materials and careful assembly.

It may be said that the company was a trifle slow getting into the automobile business. Oldsmobile started offering cars in 1901 and as an automaker would far outlast Studebaker. The Thomas B. Jeffrey Company, which evolved into the Nash Motors Company and later American Motors, began volume production of gasoline automobiles the same year Studebaker produced its first electrics. Compared to Jeffrey, Studebaker's entry was tentative and skimpy. Jeffrey, formerly a producer of bicycles, turned out a reported 1,500 Ramblers in 1902. Yet Studebaker, the major transportation company of that era, produced just 20 cars that first season, not even two percent of Jeffrey's output.

Rather than jumping with both feet into the new and exciting automotive field, Studebaker had merely dipped a toe. This was a crucial point in the formation of the auto industry, when boldness might have changed the final outcome. The industry was soon to experience growth beyond imagination and with it the emergence of powerful competitors.

The Ford Motor Company would begin operations in 1903. Its namesake was already well known in automobile circles and had produced some automobiles. The Overland automobile, ancestor of today's Jeep, also entered production in 1903.

Although these examples debuted at approximately the same time as Studebaker, there was one critical product difference that partially accounts for Studebaker's ultimate failure as an automaker. The other cars had gasoline engines while the Studebakers' were electric-powered. The plain truth is that although Studebaker was the largest vehicle builder in the world, it entered the automobile business late and with what would prove to be the wrong product. An important reason for Studebaker's eventual failure as an auto company is that it simply got off to a bad start.

Although the Studebaker cars were well made, electrics simply were not the future of motor transportation. While it's true many other companies produced electric cars, the pendulum had begun to swing away from electrics and toward the gas jobs. Admittedly, electrics had appeal; they started instantly and were quiet, smooth, and very reliable. Gasoline-engine cars, on the other hand, were more difficult to start and were noisier and smellier. Their tremendous advantage was the ability to

NO. 1358.   STUDEBAKER STANHOPE

Another Studebaker Electric model introduced in 1902 was this No. 1358 Stanhope. As can be seen, the Stanhope's body-work was much more elaborate and featured a stylishly curved dash. Notice, too, the well-upholstered seat and elegant coach lamp.

NO. 1363.   STUDEBAKER STANHOPE

Even more elegant was the No. 1363 Studebaker Stanhope with landau top to provide protection from the elements. Studebaker furnished each car with a charging plug and 15-foot cable, a tire repair kit, a tire pump, one set of tire removers, and a combination wrench.

travel long distances in a single day, at greater speeds than the electrics. A party of friends out for a pleasure drive could travel from New Haven, Connecticut, to New York City in less than half a day in a gasoline car, while an electric might take two days or more.

In addition, an electric had to be plugged in to recharge its batteries, which took hours. Heaven help the driver who ran out of juice in an area that had no electric power (there were many). The car would have to be towed home by a team of horses. Gasoline was available in many hardware and general stores, or a driver could simply take along a few extra cans to ensure he or she could make the distance. One couldn't take along extra electricity.

Changes seen by 1904 on this Studebaker Electric include spoke wheels rather than wires and cowl-mounted lamps. With a squarish hood up front and step plates to ease entry, Studebaker's horseless carriage began evolving into a distinct vehicle.

Studebaker finally got into the gasoline-powered automobile market with this 1904 model based on a Garford chassis. It was sold alternately as a Studebaker-Garford or just plain Studebaker. Gasoline cars were heavier and noisier than the electrics but could travel all day without needing a recharge, allowing motorists much greater range along with higher speeds.

Studebaker said its electric Runabout was good for a top speed of 13 miles per hour, with a range of 40 miles between charges. That was sufficient for in-town use, but many automobilists of the day were interested in faster speeds and greater distances. It wouldn't be long before the shortcomings of the electric would become obvious. When that happened, Studebaker would be forced to switch gears and come on with a different product.

The public may have preferred gasoline cars, but old John M. Studebaker didn't care for them. He'd come to enjoy the quiet electric cars, once calling the gas jobs "clumsy, dangerous, noisy brutes (that) stink to high heaven, break down at the worst possible moment and are a public nuisance." Nevertheless, management eventually realized it needed to bring a gasoline car to market. Since automotive engineers were a rare breed back then and Studebaker had none to speak of, company president Frederick Fish decided to form an alliance with an existing auto firm rather than try to design a new car from the ground up. Several firms were considered, and eventually a deal was reached with the Garford Company of Cleveland, Ohio.

Garford built automobile chassis for Studebaker beginning in 1904. The gas-engined chassis were assembled in Ohio then shipped to Studebaker's South Bend plant where the bodies were mounted (the company had already built automobile bodies for other firms). The new cars were marketed through Studebaker dealers as Studebaker-Garford autos or sometimes simply as Studebakers.

Its electric cars were still in production, so Studebaker marketed the two lines together, targeting each to a distinct audience. The electrics were touted as ideal for "convenient local use" while gas cars were perfect for "for wide-radius touring." It must have gotten a little confusing for Studebaker retailers, since in addition to the various automobiles in their display rooms, many still had horse-drawn carriages and wagons. The company's print ads sometimes referred to both the Studebaker Brothers Manufacturing Company and the Studebaker Automobile

Advances made in automobile design came swiftly. This 1905 Studebaker has room for four or five, a powerful gasoline engine, headlights, horn, cowl lights, and thickly padded seats—a perfect machine for a relaxing drive in the country.

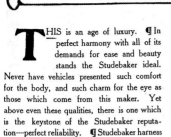
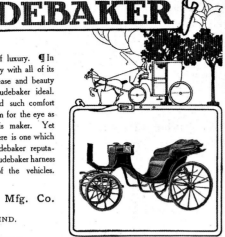

STUDEBAKER

THIS is an age of luxury. ¶ In perfect harmony with all of its demands for ease and beauty stands the Studebaker ideal. Never have vehicles presented such comfort for the body, and such charm for the eye as those which come from this maker. Yet above even these qualities, there is one which is the keystone of the Studebaker reputation—perfect reliability. ¶ Studebaker harness and accessories are typical of the vehicles.

Studebaker Bros. Mfg. Co.

SOUTH BEND, IND.

Local Agencies Everywhere.

Factory and Executive Offices:
SOUTH BEND, IND.

STUDEBAKER

THE Landaulet and other Studebaker automobile, electric and gasoline, are models of mechanical simplicity and efficiency. ¶ Lightness, speed and beauty they have, but never at the expense of safety and durability. ¶ While every feature of them is of the latest type, nothing is experimental. They employ only the most recent patent devices that have been proved worthy. Above all things, they are common sense cars, built to add to their owner's pleasure and comfort, and to the fame of Studebaker.

Studebaker Automobile Co.

SOUTH BEND, IND.

Member of Association Automobile Manufacturers

Agencies in all Principal Cities

REPOSITORIES:
New York City, Broadway and 7th Ave., at 48th St. Chicago, Ill., 378-388 Wabash Ave. Kansas City, Mo., 810-814 Walnut St. San Francisco, Cal., Corner Market and 10th Sts. Portland, Ore., 330-336 East Morrison St. Denver, Colo., Corner 15th and Blake Sts. Salt Lake City, Utah, 157-159 State St. Dallas, Texas, 317-319 Elm St.

Quality and value were the theme of this advertisement for Studebaker Brothers Manufacturing Company. It advised shoppers to "Examine any Studebaker, see how strongly it is made—what sound timber is used—how heavily it is ironed . . ." The Studebaker, it boasted, was "A wagon with a reputation."

This print ad from 1906 perfectly illustrates Studebaker's broad range of business. Studebaker Brothers Manufacturing Company produced horse-drawn vehicles, including this attractive carriage, along with harness and accessories for it, while Studebaker Automobile Company produced electric- and gasoline-powered automobiles.

Company and showed both engine-powered and horse-drawn vehicles in the same advertisement.

Studebaker purchased a minority interest in Garford, expanding it when possible so that by 1908 the company was the majority stockholder. But the Studebaker-Garfords were fairly expensive, with prices of $2,500 to $4,500 or more. Since they were so costly, production was never great, with reportedly fewer than 2,500 units built during the entire eight-year association. Meanwhile, the market was plainly moving toward lower-cost models, and other firms were stealing a lead on Studebaker. In 1908, Henry Ford introduced his all-new Model T; the line included a high-quality four-cylinder touring car priced at just $850 and a Runabout tagged at $825. The result of Ford's commitment to low-cost, high-volume production can be readily seen: The company produced more than 10,000 Ford Model T's in just the first 12 months of production.

Clearly, Studebaker needed to commit more resources to the automobile business. In 1908, the company reached an agreement with the

Powerful-looking and beautifully built, this 1908 Studebaker-Garford seven-passenger touring car was powered by a four-cylinder engine. As was common in the early days of motoring, the steering wheel was placed on the right side. This car sold new for around $3,500.

newly formed E.M.F. Company to distribute its new car through Studebaker dealers. E.M.F., formed by industry pioneers B. F. Everitt, William Metzger, and Walter Flanders, needed a large dealer network to handle the high volume of business they planned for their new car. Studebaker, on the other hand, needed a partner able to build cars in greater volume and with a lower price than Garford.

At first it seemed an ideal marriage. With Studebaker's vast distribution network behind them, the E.M.F. cars sold very well initially. However, they soon gained a reputation for problems. Wags claimed the initials stood for "Every Morning Fix-it," "Easy Mark's Favorite," and worse. Obviously, Studebaker was embarrassed to have the company's reputation marred by reports of poor quality. Other problems arose when the principals of E.M.F. began having second thoughts about the whole deal, bickering with Studebaker and even among themselves. Eventually Studebaker purchased a controlling

interest in E.M.F., determined to place its entire business on a new footing. In early 1911, E.M.F. and the Studebaker Brothers Manufacturing Company merged to become the Studebaker Corporation with J. M. Studebaker, old "Wheelbarrow Johnny" himself, as chairman and Frederick Fish as president. For a time it continued marketing automobiles under the existing brand names, but by 1913 all its cars bore the Studebaker name.

Before this happened, the company had also gotten involved with another automobile, the Flanders, produced by Walter Flanders, the F in E.M.F. The Flanders was supposed to be a low-priced car for the masses, well-built and priced less than the Ford Model T. But Henry Ford kept reducing Model T prices as production went up, so the Flanders was never able to undercut it, or sell anywhere near Ford's volume. It was a decent car, but by then Ford dominated the low-priced market. At the dawn of 1913, Flanders was gone.

This 1908–1909 Roadster has stylish lines. Note the two well-upholstered individual seats. They might be considered early bucket seats for a sporty car. Notice, too, the tiny rear "dickey" seat, sometimes referred to as a "mother-in-law seat."

By that point, Studebaker had ceased production of its electric cars, along with the E.M.F. and Studebaker-Garford brands. Only a reported 1,841 electrics had been produced in all, and 2,481 Studebaker-Garfords. Clearly, Studebaker's shotgun approach caused it to miss taking an early lead in the auto industry. Now the company had to play catch-up.

In 1913, Studebaker retailed some 24,255 cars. That was a vast improvement, but in that same year Buick sold 28,348 autos, and Willys-Overland sold more than 37,000. Ford, which in the early days didn't have the advantages of money and dealer strength Studebaker enjoyed, led the field with production of a whopping 189,000 cars. Although Studebaker held fourth place in the industry, the company had been capable of greater things. Plainly, the full might of its resources hadn't been brought to play.

But now its miscalculated forays into the auto industry were behind it. Restructured, with fresh capitalization, and in possession of proper facilities in which to manufacture cars bearing its own brand, Studebaker set out to build its position. For 1914, the company decided to standardize its automobile lineup to just two models: the Studebaker Four, priced at $1,050, and the Studebaker Six, selling for $1,575.

The company noted that sales of its vehicle line, which in Studebaker nomenclature meant horse-drawn products, were holding up well. The horse-drawn line included farm wagons, carts, delivery wagons, sprinklers, passenger vehicles, ammunition wagons, and more. The company earned profits of $1.7 million on sales of $41.4 million for 1913, which rose to profits of $4.4 million on sales of $43.4 million for 1914.

In 1915, the company boasted, "Studebaker manufactures practically all its own parts," a claim the vast majority of auto firms couldn't match. The company had a dynamic new president this year, one whose actions would shape the corporation for decades to come. Albert Russell Erskine is a historically interesting man, a dapper, hard-driving yet

For a time Studebaker also sold the Flanders automobile, a spin-off from the E.M.F. Combine. After Walter Flanders broke with his E.M.F. partners, he produced this namesake car to compete with the Ford Model T. But Henry Ford was able to keep his prices low and quality high, so the Flanders never caught on. Although this photo is labeled a 1912 Flanders Model 20, it appears identical to earlier 1909–1910 models.

ultimately tragic figure whose personal story is nearly as compelling as that of the company he ran. Although today the chairman or CEO is considered the top man in most corporations, in that era the president of a company was usually the most powerful man, and that was so with Erskine. From his elevation to the president's chair until the time he left the company, the fate of the Studebaker Corporation rested on the ideas and actions of Albert Erskine. Even after his death the decisions he'd made would continue to shape Studebaker's future.

Erskine thought lower prices would stimulate sales, and he was right. In mid-1915 Studebaker sharply reduced the price of its cars and sales volume increased 32 percent. The company netted more than $9 million in profit for 1915, and Erskine felt he was off to a good start. However, in what can be viewed as an ominous portent, the company, which usually had paid dividends of well under a million dollars, this year paid out $2,227,025 in dividends—more than the total paid in the nine-year period between 1901 to 1909! Obviously one of Erskine's core beliefs was in paying generous dividends. That was fine if he could guarantee business conditions would always be excellent.

Prices for the new 1916 Studebaker Series 16 began at $885 for a Four. Despite $1 million spent to increase car production, the

built COMPLETE in Studebaker Plants
—from the first casting to
the finished car.

It's simply a matter of insurance, that's all. Insurance of the quality that a man EXPECTS in any car that carries that name of Studebaker.

Studebaker is not satisfied merely to assemble motors and axles and parts bought from parts manufacturers, but in order to get the accuracy of fit and the balance and the harmony of operation that a car MUST have to meet Studebaker requirements, Studebaker manufactures practically all its own parts.

And so, "—because it's a Studebaker"—because this car carries a name that for 63 years has stood for the highest ideals in manufacturing—a name that has come to be a pledge of QUALITY in every detail—Studebaker MAKES SURE by manufacturing Studebaker cars COMPLETE in Studebaker plants.

Motors, gears, axles, transmissions, bodies, tops, fenders—ALL the hundreds of parts, in fact, that go to make up a car, with the exception of the tires, the horn, the electric system and such specialized equipment that is manufactured to Studebaker specifications—are designed and manufactured in Studebaker plants.

To Studebaker, this policy of COMPLETE manufacturing means the certainty that every Studebaker car lives up to the promise of its name. And to the buyer, it means a car that carries only ONE profit—because there are no parts-makers' profits in the price—and a car that can be depended upon to give SERVICE and FULL money's worth of satisfaction for every dollar of the price

—because it's a
Studebaker

in every detail from "stem to stern." But you will appreciate even better what this policy means to you when you RIDE in the Studebaker

Studebaker Features
Electric Lighting and Starting—FULL Floating Rear Axle—Timken Bearings—Safety Tread Rear Tires—One-man Type Top.

	Price in U.S.A.	Price in Canada
Studebaker ROADSTER,	$985	$1250
Studebaker FOUR,	985	1250
Studebaker LIGHT SIX,	1385	1750
Studebaker SIX (7-passenger),	1450	1825

LIGHT SIX—$1385

and see the unity, the harmony that Studebaker has been able to build into this car. When you study the balance of this Studebaker-BUILT car, and its riding comfort and its ease of control. When you feel at your own finger ends that flood of power obedient to your slightest wish.

But see it—soon. Judge its beauty, its grace of design and its elegance of finish. Get the Studebaker dealer to tell you how the upkeep cost has been cut to the bone by this same policy of COMPLETE manufacturing. And today, write for "The Story of Studebaker"—a handsomely illustrated book that tells in detail how the Studebaker is built.

STUDEBAKER DETROIT Canadian Factories, Walkerville, Ont.

By 1915 Studebaker was boasting that its cars were "Built COMPLETE in Studebaker Plants—from the first casting to the finished car." Prices of the Light Six started at $1,385, while the low-priced Studebaker Four was priced as low as $985.

company initially couldn't keep up with the tremendous demand. Yet even then the company wasn't keeping pace with the industry. In 1916 automobile sales reached 1.4 million units, of which Studebaker's share was 65,885 cars.

The Studebaker dealer network was quite large—some 6,500 strong, according to the company—or an average of just ten car sales per year each. Obviously, their selling skills needed to be brought up to par. Although Studebaker was usually ranked among the top five or ten auto companies, Buick, Ford, Essex, Willys-Overland, Chevrolet, Dodge, and others were outperforming them, with far fewer dealers.

There were also problems getting cars to market that year, caused by a nationwide shortage of freight cars. Studebaker responded by purchasing an assembly plant in Chicago and also producing cars in South Bend, to take some of the strain off its main auto plants in Michigan and ease transportation problems. Most Studebaker cars were assembled in Detroit at the time, a result of the E.M.F tie-up.

Profits fell a bit in 1916. The company had benefited in 1915 from a large influx of orders caused by the outbreak of World War I. Military orders dropped sharply for 1916, dragging profits down with them. Even so, Studebaker had net profits of $8.6 million for the year. Oddly enough, despite the profit downturn, dividends rose sharply to $3.7 million. One wonders how a responsible management could justify that.

Then came 1917 and with it a drastic drop-off in business. Volume dropped by more than $11 million, falling to just over $50 million, and profits shrank to just $3.5 million. Management stated the reason behind the drop was a vastly reduced demand for the four-cylinder Studebaker that occurred after the company pushed through a substantial increase in its price. The resulting high inventories had to be financed by bank loans, which reached $13 million at one point and were a drag on earnings.

It's surprising a company of Studebaker's size didn't have more cash on hand. In seven years it had earned more than $30 million in profits, yet at year-end it had less than $3 million in cash. More surprising, dividends were only reduced to $2.8 million, or half a million more than in 1915 when a $9 million profit was reported. Erskine obviously wasn't basing dividends on profit levels. That same year, John Mohler Studebaker, the last of the original founding brothers, passed away at the age of 83.

The company had spent quite a bit of money on the design and engineering of a completely new line of cars for introduction as 1918 models, and fine machines they were! Developed by Fred Zeder, Owen Skelton, and Carl Breer—the same three brilliant engineers who went on to create Walter Chrysler's original namesake car—the 1918 Studebaker line included a five-passenger four-cylinder model on a 112-inch wheelbase priced at $895, a 119-inch five-passenger six at $1,295, and a seven-passenger six on a long 126-inch wheelbase, tagged at $1,695. Albert Erskine bragged they were "beautiful in design, thoroughly modern, will undoubtedly enjoy great popularity and be sold as fast as we can make them. . . ." But sales were lower than expected. The government's need for military equipment limited the company's

For 1918 Studebaker offered a 112-inch-wheelbase five-passenger four-cylinder model priced at $895, a 119-inch five-passenger six at $1,295, and a 126-inch-wheelbase seven-passenger six for $1,695. In advertisements the Big Six was extolled as *"beautiful in design, thoroughly modern, mechanically right."* However, military needs preempted civilian, so the company produced only 18,270 automobiles that year.

This rare, unrestored vehicle is a 1913 "AA35" center door sedan, reportedly the only one known to exist. Owner Larry Leek.

production to only 18,270 automobiles. Half of the 58,830 horse-drawn vehicles Studebaker produced that year (a number vastly greater than automobile production, one should note) went to war contracts, and the firm also produced large numbers of gun carriages, mine anchors, shell parts, wheel hubs, and artillery wheels. When the armistice was signed that year, Studebaker needed to expend large amounts of money to convert its plants back to civilian production. The company noted proudly that in a little over four years it had delivered more than $37 million in war goods.

Before his death, J. M. Studebaker was able to exert his influence on a critically important decision. Automobile production had always been centered in Detroit, where the E.M.F. and Flanders plants were established. But when it became clear that Studebaker's business would eventually be devoted almost exclusively to automobiles, J. M. spoke to Albert Erskine. J. M. was of the old school that held a successful man owed a certain debt to those who had helped make his success. At heart, "Wheelbarrow Johnny" felt as one with the men who earned their daily bread working in his shops, and he worried what might happen to his South Bend employees when the horse-drawn business was no longer viable. The company would eventually need to construct an additional auto plant. Why not build it in South Bend?

He explained his thoughts to Erskine, who promised that when Studebaker put up a new automobile factory the company would build it in South Bend so those workers could remain part of the Studebaker family. Work began in 1916 and continued in fits and starts as wartime needs dictated so that by the time of the armistice, less than one-third of the plant was completed. It was designed with a capacity of 100,000 cars per year. Meanwhile, the Detroit plants continued producing cars.

The Light Six was called "the ideal five-passenger car." With its quick acceleration and quality construction, it was a popular model. Note that Studebaker had plants in Detroit, Michigan, South Bend, Indiana, and Walkerville, Ontario.

The New
Studebaker
LIGHT SIX

Prosperity soared at Studebaker in 1919. Sales volume rose to $66 million, with net profits of $9.3 million. The company began an orderly exit from the horse-drawn vehicle market, liquidating its investments in all horse-drawn vehicle lines except farm wagons and farm trucks. The plant space thus saved would be devoted to production of automotive parts and closed bodies for automobiles.

For 1920, the Studebaker line included the Light Six produced in South Bend and the Detroit-built Special Six and Big Six models. The company reported mixed results for the year. On one hand, sales volume set a record at $90 million, up $24 million from the prior year. But on the other hand, profits rose just half a million, to $9.8 million.

There were growing signs of a problem in Erskine's philosophy of business. Despite the small increase in profits, management increased the dividend on common stock by $1,837,000, which meant there was less money left over for use in the business compared to the prior year. Albert Erskine believed that generous dividends strengthened the price of the company's stock and was, after all, what stockholders were entitled to. His philosophy meant less capital was available for growing the business. Although Studebaker became larger, its rate of growth wasn't as great as that of some of its competitors, and in the auto business, size is everything. Paying out generous dividends also meant less capital available as a reserve against hard times. Apparently Erskine didn't think Studebaker would ever see hard times again. To his eyes, the future held only greater success.

A watershed event occurred in May 1920. The company decided to liquidate the balance of its farm wagon business while it could still do so at a reasonable price. Much of its inventory went out through regular trade channels, and the firm incurred a loss of just more than $700,000 after terms on certain deals were adjusted. The remaining stock of farm wagons was sold to the Kentucky Wagon Manufacturing Company. Thus ended production of the famed products in which Studebaker and its predecessors had been engaged for 62 years. From that point on, the success or failure of the Studebaker Corporation would depend on the automobile business.

With the new direction, the company flourished. Sales were up again in 1921 reaching $96.6 million, and profits broke the $10 million mark for the first time. Wholesale sales of Studebaker cars (that is, sales to its dealers) were 66,643 units compared to 51,474 the prior year, representing a handsome 29.5 percent increase. The company noted that after removing sales of Ford and Studebaker cars, total industry sales had reached just a mere 55 percent of the prior year's total. An enormous increase for Ford, plus Studebaker's good showing, were responsible for most of the industry's total sales increase for the year. It was something to crow about, as was the proud boast that Studebaker's spare parts sales were down 12 percent from 1919 despite

The top's landau irons give this 1921 Studebaker Light Six two-passenger coupe a certain smartness and taste. Some sources question whether or not this model ever went into production. This appears to be an artist's rendering rather than a photo of an actual car.

the large increase in vehicle population. The company termed it "direct proof of the quality and durability of Studebaker cars." Good cars they were, too, thanks to sound engineering aimed at eliminating any remaining speck of the poor service reputation caused by the E.M.F. cars.

The company was proud of its reputation for caring for its workers and this year boasted that of 13,065 employees, 9,305 received checks on the anniversary of their employment, 4,402 got a week's vacation with pay, and the dependents of 12 deceased employees received insurance payments. In addition, 2,830 employees owned stock in the company. Albert Erskine and the board of directors also noted with regret the death of Alonzo Hepburn, characterized as "a staunch friend of the corporation and a valued associate director." Such official tributes are not uncommon in annual reports; however, company management had not made any similar mention in the annual report when company founder J. M.

Studebaker passed away four years earlier. Certainly it would seem they owed a lot more to J. M. than to Mr. Hepburn.

The early 1920s were golden years. Studebaker focused entirely on the automobile business, increasing production and making money by the barrel. Sales climbed to $133 million in 1922, and net profits shot to $18 million, both new records. Despite increased plant capacity, demand continued to outpace production. By March, output was up to 440 units per day, but demand still surpassed availability by thousands of cars. Studebaker missed out selling many more cars simply because it hadn't increased production enough. It's easy to see why that happened. Sales for 1922 totaled 110,269 cars, topping 1920's sales by 114 percent. Not many managers could anticipate that sales would more than double in two years, though the ones that did profited greatly.

The 1920–1921 model lineup introduced the lovely and powerful Studebaker Big Six four-door sedan. This seven-passenger automobile featured a large window area. With a price around $2,200, it offered tremendous value for the money.

In a fit of generosity—there's no better way to phrase it—the company declared a stock dividend of $15 million payable to shareholders of record as of December 16, 1922. This was no doubt welcomed by stockholders, but it probably would have been better for them and the company if it had gone toward building additional production capacity or strengthening the dealer network. Although Studebaker was making money hand over fist, there was no guarantee the situation would last forever.

A prudent manager invests in the business first and then pays reasonable dividends over a span of time. Nash Motors, a far younger and smaller firm whose 1923 dollar volume was about one-third of Studebaker's, kept about $8 million more in cash and bonds on hand than the South Bend firm and had essentially no bank debt. An auto executive remarked around this time that sales were essentially a product of production,

meaning a company could sell as many cars as it could build, and that was true for some firms. The real test would come when the automobile market became difficult. For now, the Roaring Twenties were, well, roaring.

The company set another record for 1923: Sales topped $166 million, up 24.8 percent, though profits grew a mere 1.4 percent. Management pointed out that sales of Studebaker cars during 1923 brought in more revenue than the horse-drawn business had done in the entire 68 years the company was involved in that business.

In 1924, Studebaker attained sixth place in industry sales, behind Ford, Buick, Chevrolet, Dodge, and Willys-Overland. Erskine visited Europe, where the company's products sold well despite high tariffs. The European branches were one part of a not-inconsequential business conducted outside the United States that contributed to Studebaker's sales and profits. Studebaker had long

The strikingly attractive 1927 Big Six Victoria on a 120-inch wheelbase was as handsome a car as anyone could want. Notice the stylish details, including the landau bars and hood ornament.

maintained an auto plant in Walkerville, Ontario, Canada, which supplied that country as well as other Sterling markets. The company also had an affiliate in Rio de Janeiro. While in Europe, Erskine gathered information about the industry and buyer preferences. He asked dealers for input on the sort of car they'd most like to have in their showrooms. Erskine planned to produce a new small car in America that could sell in overseas markets while also competing with America's low-priced giants Ford and Chevrolet. Erskine took a collection of ideas back to South Bend for a discussion with his engineers. From this, the new car would be developed.

Meanwhile, on September 14, the company introduced a complete line of all-new cars consisting of 15 models on three different wheelbases. They were some of the best-looking cars on the road and a dramatic improvement. Public interest was high. In the first three days the new cars were

displayed, two million people visited Studebaker showrooms and some 9,000 orders were placed. But they came too late to salvage 1924; sales volume for the year fell by more than $30 million and profits by about $4.5 million. In spite of this, dividends remained the same as before: $7.5 million.

The new cars turned everything back in Studebaker's favor during 1925, with sales of some 134,000 units reported. Dollar volume rose to $161 million, and profits were $16.6 million. That was still down compared to 1923, yet the dividend payout actually increased to $9.8 million, continuing a disturbing trend. During the year, a young executive named Paul G. Hoffman was promoted to vice president of sales. Although then relatively unknown, in time he would become a legendary figure in Studebaker lore.

Hit with a variety of extraordinary expenses during 1926, Studebaker experienced a downturn in profitability. The aging

Here is the Studebaker Commander Sport Roadster for 1928. This stylish two-passenger car had the kind of sporty lines that appealed to young people. The wire wheels shown here were an extra-cost option. By 1928 Studebaker had moved most of its Detroit operations to South Bend, where the company had new buildings erected at a cost of nearly $1 million.

Detroit plants were vacated, with most manufacturing and engineering moved to South Bend. Savings would eventually accrue from this, but in the meantime the cost of closing and moving everything was quite large. The company also purchased 800 acres of land west of South Bend for construction of a new proving grounds. In addition, there were the normal expenses of introducing new features and innovations into the car lineup.

Probably the largest expense was the cost of engineering and tooling an all-new small car to be introduced for 1927. This was the European-influenced model envisioned by Erskine some two years earlier. It was to be Studebaker's entry into the lower-priced market, and the company had great hopes for it. Albert Erskine predicted that 1927 "will prove to be the most prosperous in our history."

Announced in October 1926, the new car didn't use the Studebaker name; instead, it bore the name *Erskine*. Board members claimed it was their idea, but even so Erskine had to give his approval, an embarrassingly immodest display of self-tribute by the company's president. The new Erskine rode a 107-inch wheelbase and was powered by a 146-cid six-cylinder engine producing 40 horsepower. Although small, the Erskine was quite stylish. Prices ranged from $945 to $995, which was a rather high price tag for a small car of that era. Ford Model T prices began under $400, a Chevrolet coupe could be bought for $625, and even Hudson's popular Essex was well under the Erskine's price. Although it did well in Europe—the company claimed overseas sales were up 68.8 percent—in America it encountered resistance to its lofty price, and sales weren't strong.

This aerial view shows the main plants of the Studebaker Corporation in 1931. The country was in the grip of the Great Depression, and sales of new cars were falling. In 1931 Studebaker's net profits were just $399,555.

689-8-30

When the Erskine failed to meet expectations, management engaged in a bit of spin. In 1926, company executives had stated that Erskine seemed sure to do "big business." But by the end of 1927 the company was downplaying the Erskine's importance, referring to it now as merely a "filler" (that was the word they used) in the Studebaker line, recognizing it was unlikely ever to be a volume leader. Its failure affected Studebaker's overall performance for 1927. Contrary to Albert Erskine's prediction of record sales, the company reported a 5.3 percent drop in sales and an 8.5 percent decrease in profits. Management shrugged and paid out more than $9 million in dividends. Studebaker celebrated its 75th anniversary on February 16, 1927.

In December, the company introduced the gorgeous new Studebaker President Straight Eight, and the cars were an instant success. In addition, the Dictator and Commander lines saw many improvements, giving the company a solid base for resuming growth in 1928. That growth was fairly impressive; the company sold its dealers 136,205 cars, a gain of 16.7 percent, though it noted that again this year the growth came mainly from export sales. Profits of nearly $14 million were up 16.8 percent. Dividends of nearly $10 million were paid to shareholders.

Albert Erskine called 1928 "one of the most important of the entire 76 years of Studebaker's history" from the standpoint both of achievement and groundwork for future progress. With the exception of a few departments, the balance of the Detroit operations were moved to South Bend, where the company had erected new buildings at a cost of nearly $1 million. The total expense of the move and consolidation was close to $6 million. The company paid out $9.3 million in dividends on common stock and more than half a million in dividends on preferred stock. All in all, it was a substantial outpouring of funds. Of all the cash that flowed into Studebaker that year, only a mere $345,850 went into the company's earned surplus account at year-end.

Albert Erskine said the new Studebaker cars debuting for 1929 were the finest the company had ever offered. They were exceptionally good-looking and good performers, too. In fact, that year Studebaker cars established 160 official speed and distance records.

Prosperity reigned in America in early 1929. Erskine wanted the company to have an entry in the burgeoning prestige market. Building a name and reputation among luxury car buyers takes time, so Erskine decided to buy an existing firm. Studebaker purchased a large interest in the prestigious Pierce-Arrow Motor Car Company

During 1931 Studebaker, like other automakers, struggled with a feeble economy, buyers' fears, and economic uncertainty. Ironically, it was during this period that the company was turning out some of the best automobiles it had ever produced. This 1931 President Eight Sport Roadster was fast, good-looking, and well built.

and assumed management of it. The idea itself was good; the timing, unfortunately, was not.

Things certainly got off to a good start. Studebaker reorganized Pierce-Arrow, strengthened its financial position, and got a new line of Straight Eights into production at the rate of 50 cars a day, with plans to double that number within a few months. The company stated "the outlook is bright for substantial profits in 1929 for both Pierce-Arrow and Studebaker."

But in 1929 the stock market crashed. Although it occurred toward the end of the year, sales for the year were down considerably. Dollar volume fell 18 percent to $145 million, and net profits fell 5.7 percent to just under $12 million. Yet despite the sales drop and the frightening events on Wall Street, the company paid out $9.5 million in cash dividends.

The first full year of what became known as the Great Depression was 1930. As was the case with virtually every auto company that year, Studebaker suffered a severe drop in business. Trying to put the best

In the depths of the Great Depression, this lovely 1932 Studebaker, a personification of the good life, was beyond the means of most Americans. Owner: Paul Wichterman. *Photo courtesy John Katz*

face on it, the company reported that Pierce-Arrow's 19 percent sales decrease was the best showing of any maker in the auto industry.

Sales for Studebaker fell 31.8 percent, nearly matching the overall industry drop of 32.3 percent. Registration figures showed Studebaker rising to fifth place in sales. The company's dollar volume fell 40.8 percent, to $86 million, and net profits to just $527,000. Amazingly, the company proceeded to pay out $7.3 million in dividends on common stock, paid out of profits from previous years. Erskine felt the downturn would be short-lived and the economy would soon rebound.

One of Studebaker's problems was that the Erskine, which was renamed the Studebaker Six in May, wasn't selling well.

Although the company had earlier produced small numbers of trucks, this year it jumped into the market in a big way with a line of Studebaker trucks and commercial cars ranging in price from $695 to

The exquisite instrument panel on the 1932 Studebaker lends added class to this lovely car. *Photo courtesy John Katz*

The sad fact is that during the Depression, Studebaker was producing some of the best-looking cars it had ever built, but economic uncertainty kept sales low. This 1932 Studebaker coupe has beautiful lines. Owner: Paul Wichterman. *Photo courtesy John Katz*

$4,375, along with a line of six-cylinder Pierce-Arrow heavy-duty truck chassis priced from $2,950 to $7,000.

For many workers, these were difficult times. In a gesture of kindness, the company made small personal loans to several thousand employees struggling to make ends meet now that most were working only part-time. Employment fell by more than 6,000.

Things got worse. In 1931 sales fell another 25 percent, to $64 million, and net profits were just $399,555. Sales held up initially; during the first three quarters business was steady and profitable. But the fourth quarter was the worst the industry had experienced in a decade. Studebaker dealers took just 10,241 vehicles, causing the company to suffer substantial losses.

Erskine still thought prosperity was just around the corner. The company introduced a new low-priced car for 1932, the Rockne Six, named for Notre Dame's famous football coach. Priced from $585 to $840, the Rockne was exactly the sort of car the Erskine should have been: low-priced and designed for American roads. In addition to the Rockne, the company offered the Studebaker Six priced at $840 to $1,090, the Studebaker Eight for $980 to $2,095, and the Pierce-Arrow line priced from $2,495 to $4,500. Studebaker trucks were $695 to $1,540, and the sturdy Pierce-Arrow trucks were again priced from $2,950 to $7,000.

For 1932, Pierce-Arrow introduced one of the greatest cars of all time, the Pierce-Arrow Twelve. With the Pierce-Arrow, the handsome Studebakers, and the low-priced Rockne, Erskine was confident in the future. Despite the ravaged economy, the company authorized payment of $2.3 million in dividends to stockholders.

There certainly was nothing wrong with the products. Rockne was a decent car; the Pierce-Arrow Twelve a great one. The only problem was that neither one was right for the times. With millions of out-of-work Americans standing in bread lines it was unfashionable to be seen in something like the Pierce-Arrow Twelve, which cost more than some people's homes. And the Rockne probably would have been a resounding success if it had appeared in 1924, but by 1931 there were few people who could buy a car, and those who could were reluctant to gamble on a new, untried make.

People would remember 1932 as one of the worst years of their lives, a time when even the kindest person might secretly hope that an older worker would die so a job would open up. As bad as it had been,

the Depression grew much worse. Many more people were thrown out of work, factories closed, and everywhere hope was fading. Studebaker production was 42 percent below the awful 1931 numbers, the company managed to sell only 49,868 vehicles, and for the first time in its history the corporation recorded a loss. The loss was staggering—more than $8 million. Yet incredibly, even with that sobering news, the company paid out more than half a million dollars in dividends. Another company would have drawn the line, but Erskine continued to believe that paying out dividends was a sign of corporate strength. It was, he held, a way to help Studebaker stock retain its value.

Regardless, by this point one must ask how the board of directors could justify paying dividends when it was losing money, or earlier how it justified paying out more than the company earned. Studebaker was known for generous dividends; that was one reason why its stock was popular with investors, but the end of the road was fast appearing. Although Erskine must bear most of the responsibility, a good measure of blame also should be assigned to the company's directors, who apparently rubber-stamped anything Erskine asked. More puzzling is Fred Fish, longtime Studebaker chairman and member of the Studebaker family. With his vast business expertise, it's surprising that Fish hadn't taken action to halt the continuing outflow of funds.

The shame of all this is that Studebaker was producing some of its greatest cars ever. In prosperous times the cars would have sold like mad, boosting company profits to new highs. Instead, Studebaker was quickly unraveling. It's the responsibility of management to secure and maintain the health of the corporation, to strengthen and safeguard it. Management has an almost sacred responsibility with stockholders to protect their investment. Yet by 1932, Studebaker had little cash left, and things were getting worse. Searching for a way out of their troubles, Erskine and his directors cast about for a partner with which to merge, one with enough cash to keep them afloat until things turned around. They settled on the White Motor Company of Ohio, a producer of commercial trucks.

White was a much smaller company than Studebaker, and it, too, was losing money. But White had a fairly substantial amount of cash on hand, good liquidity, and was also looking for a partner. Since Studebaker was already in the truck business, merging with White could effect substantial savings in production costs, which would benefit both parties. And Studebaker's large dealer network could help increase White's

The body of this 1933 Studebaker Six Suburban Model 56 wagon was built by Cantrell, a Long Island, New York, builder of specialty bodies. Because station wagons were expensive, low-volume products, many automakers relied on outside firms to supply the bodies for their station wagon models.

sales volume. But most of all, merging with White would bring Studebaker enough cash to stay afloat until prosperity finally arrived.

In the later part of 1932, Erskine authorized a deal to merge with White. Initially it was approved, and the company's annual report that year showed a consolidated balance sheet. It appears that of the $9.6 million in cash reported by the combined firms, about $7 million came from White. However, in the end, a small group of White investors blocked the deal, citing an Ohio law prohibiting out-of-state companies from merging with an Ohio company and taking their working capital out of state. It stalled things long enough for Studebaker to reach the crisis stage. With no money left and large loans outstanding, the company was on the very edge of catastrophe. To save it, on March 18, 1933,

the directors were forced to, as they put it, consent to receivership. Stated less delicately, the company was going into bankruptcy.

Most Americans view corporate bankruptcy as the end of the line, a sign of complete failure. But in many cases it can signal a new beginning. The big advantage of bankruptcy is that it can, in certain circumstances, provide protection from creditors, allowing time for a company to devise a plan to save the business. This ability to operate under the protection of the bankruptcy court has saved many firms. At the time, Studebaker's management believed the company would ultimately emerge from bankruptcy as a strong, going concern. The fact that no other automobile firm had ever done so was perhaps not known by them.

Studebaker produced a wide variety of trucks and commercial cars during the 1930s. One of the best-looking was the Coupe Express. This beautiful example is a 1937 model. *Photo courtesy Mike Mueller*

CHAPTER THREE

1934-1945
The Champion that Saved Studebaker

I n the scorched cauldron of the Great Depression and bankruptcy, a new Studebaker Corporation was created. It would be a leaner company than before, but proud to have survived and anxious to begin the job of regaining its former prominence.

To better understand what Studebaker faced at that time, it's necessary to understand how receivership laws work. In cases of corporate bankruptcy, there are generally two main options available: liquidation, which is known as Chapter 7, or reorganization, known as Chapter 11.

In Chapter 7 liquidation the company is dissolved. A court-appointed trustee arranges for the sale of all the company's assets, and all proceeds are used to pay off creditors to the greatest extent possible. Since the company isn't being sold as a going concern, its assets, are generally worth a great deal less than before, sometimes pennies on the dollar. In most cases creditors receive only a portion of what they're owed.

In Chapter 11, a company is sheltered from creditors for a certain period to give receivers—individuals whom the court has placed in charge of the company's affairs—time to formulate a plan for satisfying the company's debts, or some portion of them, and to reorganize the company so that it can emerge from bankruptcy with a hope of successfully resuming operations.

When Studebaker entered receivership in March 1933, it was thought that perhaps Albert Erskine and Frederick Fish would remain at the helm, but that was not to be. The misguided fiscal policies of the former and the lack of prudent oversight of the latter doomed any chance of either remaining in power. In the end, the court appointed Studebaker executives Paul G. Hoffman and Harold S. Vance along with Ashton Bean of the White Motor Company as receivers, to oversee the company's affairs and formulate a plan for reorganizing the firm. Hoffman became president of Studebaker, and Vance became chairman.

Frederick Fish resigned. Albert Erskine did, too, his life's work in ruins. A shattered man, within weeks he would shoot himself to death in his home, leaving behind a note bearing the sad message, "I cannot go on any longer." Erskine had flown high in the corporate world, and for a time he enjoyed tremendous success. His anguish at finally realizing how his policies had drained the lifeblood from Studebaker must have been acute. However one may feel about his mistakes and errors of judgment, Erskine paid the ultimate price for having made them, and in all of corporate history there are few sadder tales.

There certainly was nothing wrong with the cars the company produced. They were well built and handsome. Commander and President

Designer Raymond Loewy was the man responsible for the stunning good looks of the 1938 Studebakers. This lovely 1938 President Coupe has very stylish lines. Notice how the headlamps are beginning to merge into the fender rather than being carried in separate pods like so many other cars of that era.

models featured sloping radiator grilles, vee'd bumpers, and attention-grabbing large headlamps. With wire wheels or steel air wheels, side-mounted spares, and gently flowing fenders, they were instantly recognizable as Studebaker products. They had plenty of appeal and a large, loyal dealer force that could sell them if someone, somewhere, would inspire them to do so. Things were at a standstill; what was needed to get sales moving again were signs that the company was going to continue on, that it wasn't simply going to roll over and die.

Production was halted for a time, but Hoffman and Vance soon got it going again. Funds were scraped together for an advertising campaign to reassure the public that the company, though down, was far from out.

"Studebaker Carries On" the ad said, explaining that the company's plants were back in production. Advertisements carried Studebaker's message of hope and determination to millions of households, letting everyone know the company wasn't going to fade away. Many Americans, who were also struggling with the effects of the Depression, felt a sense of kinship with Studebaker as it faced its woes with quiet resolve.

A broad-ranging sales program was instituted to spur salespeople to new efforts. Automobile sales resumed on a fairly strong level as Hoffman and Vance struggled to rebuild the company. They sold Pierce-Arrow at a huge loss because doing so eliminated a continuing money drain while bringing in much-needed cash. The Rockne was dropped; production would focus on Studebaker-branded products. America's economy, however, remained stuck in a depression. Studebaker lost $4.8 million in 1933 and $1.46 million in 1934.

Hoffman and Vance eventually came up with a plan for reorganizing the company with an infusion of new capital. The White truck stock was sold, and White went its separate way, the promise it once held for Studebaker ending up little more than an unfortunate footnote attached to the company's history. How differently things might have gone if the White deal had worked out! But fate conspired to prevent it, and Studebaker was forced to go, phoenix-like, through an agonizing ritual of death and rebirth.

Studebaker's suppliers and dealers would suffer a great deal of worry before the company finally emerged from the court's protection as a new, reorganized corporation. But however much time they spent fretting about the reorganization, corporate liquidation—the only alternative—would have been far more devastating. In that scenario, the company's assets would have been sold off in an atmosphere much like a fire sale.

To fully understand the ramifications of bankruptcy liquidation, it's necessary to understand where each group of stakeholders (those having an interest or "stake" in the company's well-being) sits in the feeding line when assets are divided up. First in line are creditors, those persons or institutions holding company debt. These would include any banks that loaned money to the company, plus holders of corporate bonds or other debt instruments. Next in line are companies to whom money is owed for materials, supplies, and services. Last on the list are stockholders because they're considered owners of the company. This class gets whatever's left after the claims of the first two groups have been satisfied. Often there is nothing left.

Judge Thomas Slick of the U.S. District Court was a South Bend man, and he understood how liquidation would devastate his already struggling city. He had come to believe in Hoffman and Vance's abilities and was confident they were up to the job of nursing Studebaker back to health. With an eye to the disparate hopes of workers, management, stockholders, and creditors, Slick approved the reorganization. In doing so he stated his belief that "to reorganize under [this] plan . . . will put the new company in a strong financial position and save something for both classes of stockholders, eliminate all present creditors, and bids fair to save a large and useful industry. . . . In these times of industrial unrest it would seem that the court must consider these questions seriously

before wrecking an industry by putting it on the auction block. [This] plan is not perfect, but it is the best—in fact, the only feasible one offered." Creditors received partial payments and stock in the new company. Those who held shares of preferred stock were given stock in the new company. Holders of Studebaker common stock got relatively little; mainly they were granted certain subscription rights to stock in the new Studebaker company.

The new Studebaker Corporation was incorporated in January 1935. For the calendar year, the company sold 45,068 cars and trucks to its dealers, a fair start but not enough to meet expenses. The new Studebaker lost $2.58 million in 1935.

But hope was in the air. New models were introduced for 1936 in two series, utilizing two wheelbases rather than three as before. The new Studebakers were fine-looking cars and well priced. The new Dictator ranged in price from $665 to $775, while the President was tagged from $965 to $1,065. In introducing them, management said it was influenced by knowledge of the "importance of re-establishing Studebaker products in public favor to such an extent that the larger volume . . . considered essential might be obtained." They explained that the reason they set prices so low was "so that every layman would recognize that Studebaker cars and trucks represent the greatest value per dollar in their respective fields."

Bargain pricing and a simplified model lineup worked the trick. Sales shot up dramatically as buyers flocked to Studebaker showrooms. Wholesale sales to dealers totaled 91,999 cars and trucks, more than double the previous years' sales. Dollar volume rose to nearly $69 million, and the company reported a profit of $2.1 million, equivalent to $1.01 per share.

What Vance and Hoffman had accomplished was nearly miraculous. In addition to the sales and profit successes, Studebaker registrations increased 71 percent for 1936 versus a 24 percent average increase for the industry. The assorted vultures and corporate undertakers that had been waiting to lay the company in its grave would have to put away their shovels for now. Studebaker was going to live.

The 1936 cars, while perhaps not quite as elegant as some of their predecessors, were stylish enough with graceful, flowing lines in tune with popular tastes. The Dictator Six rode a 116-inch wheelbase, while the President series boasted a 125-inch chassis.

There is no way one can understate the importance of the new Studebaker Champion introduced for 1939. It breathed new life into the struggling company and brought it to new heights of production.

STUDEBAKER CHAMPION CLUB SEDAN

STUDEBAKER COMMANDER CRUISING SEDAN

STUDEBAKER PRESIDENT COUPE

The cars returned for 1937 in the same two series with revamped styling. Sales continued to rise throughout most of the year until the fourth quarter of 1937, when the economy stumbled and sales dropped off precipitously. A 37 percent drop in sales during the last three months of the year reduced Studebaker's profits to just $811,000, despite having produced some 91,475 units, only about 500 fewer than in 1936. The downturn during the last three months was so sharp the company ended up losing money on each car sold during that period.

Studebaker dropped the Dictator name for 1938. Years earlier the word's original definition, a figure of supreme authority appointed in times of emergency, had been better known. Now, with Hitler and Mussolini beginning to strut across the world stage, the name had a connotation far different from the original. It was time to retire it.

Thus for 1938, the Studebaker cars got some new names. The line now consisted of three series: Commander, State Commander, and State President. Styling was great, and the cars should have sold well, but the economy was in a slump. In fact, the downturn of late 1937 was the beginning of a mini-recession, and commerce everywhere dropped sharply. The recession carried over into 1938, and many people feared it was the start of a new depression. But in the end, it was relatively short-lived, and by year end the economy picked up again.

In the meantime, however, the drastic fall-off in sales caused the auto industry to suffer a very bad year. Studebaker sales to dealers for 1938 tumbled to just 52,605 units, and dollar volume amounted to $43.7 million. There was no way to squeeze a profit out of those slim numbers, and the corporation lost $1.7 million for the year.

For 1940 Studebaker offered three ranges of automobile aimed at three distinct price classes. The volume seller was the low-priced Champion (top), while the medium-priced Commander offered more room, style, and power at a moderate price increase. The President was the top of the line, a beautiful and powerful prestige car.

The 1942 Champion Deluxstyle Coupe. The Deluxstyle series included more chrome trim, though of course after the attack on Pearl Harbor chrome use was severely restricted. The two-tone paint and rear wheel skirts add a lot to the beauty of this automobile.

In that idyllic time before Pearl Harbor, one could daydream about lovely summer days and beautiful cars like this 1942 Champion Deluxstyle Cruising sedan.

The only good news was that Studebaker's drop in retail sales wasn't nearly as severe as many, and the company didn't suffer as harsh a financial loss as some other firms. The company even managed to increase its share of the market. While the auto industry's total production fell 48 percent, Studebaker's fell by only 43 percent; bad enough, though it could have been much worse. Studebaker now ranked 10th among the country's automakers, up from 13th.

Vance and Hoffman had recognized from the beginning that what the company needed more than anything was greater sales volume. They realized that higher sales volume was difficult to obtain in the limited arena in which they were selling. However, just a few rungs below them on the price ladder was the enormous "low-priced" segment dominated by Chevrolet, Ford, and Plymouth. Roughly two-thirds of all car sales in America came from that segment. If Studebaker could field a competitive car, the company could grow sales volume much more quickly than trying to improve its relative position in the crowded medium and upper price ranges.

So Hoffman and Vance set their engineers to work designing a new car to compete directly with the "Low-Price Three." It was a difficult task because Chevy, Ford, and Plymouth had the advantage of enormous purchasing power that gave them a significant cost advantage on nearly every component used, along with large-scale production capacity, which drove per-unit costs down to a minimum. Because it wouldn't initially have as much sales volume as other makes, the per unit amortization figure would be much higher. Yet Sudebaker was forced to price their car close to the others if they hoped to be competitive. In addition to the problems of cost, there was the simple fact that if Studebaker didn't offer customers something more than just a me-too car, buyers would have little reason to purchase a Studebaker over a better-known brand. Human nature being what it is, if customers didn't feel it was smarter to buy a Studebaker, they'd probably take the safe bet: a car from an established brand, such as Ford, Chevy, or Plymouth.

It was, in other words, one hell of a gamble for a struggling independent company to make. But Vance and Hoffman felt it was the only way for Studebaker to gain entrance to the big leagues of automaking. The Engineering Department stepped up to the task and quickly proved that it still had the greatness for which Studebaker was renowned.

Studebaker's big military trucks stand out in all the major war zones

IN virtually every theater of this global war, mighty military trucks produced by Studebaker are moving the men and supplies of the United Nations.

From the Alcan highway to the Russian front, from Africa to China, tens of thousands of these big Studebakers have been writing brilliant new pages of transport history.

The stand-up stamina of these rugged Studebaker trucks is nothing new. It's as old as the Studebaker business. It goes back more than 91 years to the days when the Studebaker brothers made the phrase, "give more than you promise," the watchword for all Studebaker activities.

Studebaker today is one of the world's leading builders of big, multiple-drive military trucks—and is also producing great quantities of powerful Wright Cyclone engines for the Boeing Flying Fortress as well as much other vital war matériel.

Send 10¢ for a beautiful reprint of this Flying Fortress painting—This dramatic picture of a Flying Fortress is available in 24x22 inch size on a special stock suitable for framing, free from advertising. Address Studebaker, South Bend, Indiana, enclosing 10¢ to cover mailing cost.

During World War II Studebaker again served its country as it had in the Civil War, Spanish American War, and World War I. Nearly 200,000 Studebaker trucks were produced for the U.S. military and its allies.

A leaner, tougher Studebaker met the Big Three head-on, with a product that was stylish and roomy yet engineered with less weight to provide outstanding fuel economy and low operation cost. Every component was designed for durability and lower weight. Careful design and engineering resulted in a car that was far lighter than the average family sedan, providing benefits like longer tire life, easier handling, better fuel economy, and a reduction in operating cost. In fact, the new Studebaker boasted the lowest operating cost of any standard-size automobile in America. The company named its new small car the Champion, and that's exactly what it was. It

One of the more unusual commercial cars produced by Studebaker is this interesting 1940 Coupe Express.

championed excellent economy and sensible motoring. It became a champion to the thousands of owners who loved its outstanding service. And it became a champion to the company that created it.

The new low-price contender came along at just the right time, pulling Studebaker out of the doldrums and injecting it with excitement and energy. It's perhaps not a stretch to say it saved the company, for in order to survive, Studebaker needed to grow, and with the new Champion, the company began to flourish.

Champion production began in February 1939, and the new car was introduced to the public that April. Champion was priced toward the upper end of the low-price class, with a basic Custom coupe priced at $660, a two-door Club Sedan tagged at $700, and a four-door sedan

at $740. Deluxe models ranged from $720 to $800. For comparison, a new Chevrolet started around $628 for a coupe, $648 for a two-door sedan, and $689 for a four-door. A Ford coupe could be had for as little as $599. But the Studebaker cars' careful engineering eliminated unnecessary weight so that the Champion was 300 to 600 pounds lighter than its competitors, giving it good performance and class-leading fuel economy.

Management referred to the new Champion as "a low-priced car that will rank high in appearance and performance and afford the owner the lowest operating cost of any car in its class." The car was all that and more. Studebaker now had a highly competitive entry in the biggest market segment of them all.

Production soared! Management boasted that during the 1939 fiscal year, sales to dealers more than doubled to 114,196 cars and

1942 Studebaker Skyway Series Commander Land Cruiser photographed at Great Lakes Naval Training Station, Great Lakes, Illinois.

This big, beautiful sedan is the 1942 Studebaker Skyway Commander Land Cruiser. In late 1941 and early 1942, ads often depicted Studebaker cars with military personnel.

commercial vehicles. Dollar volume for the corporation climbed to $81 million, and a net profit of $2.9 million was recorded, which represented a $4.6 million turnaround from 1938's big loss. The Champion was a midyear introduction, so the numbers, excellent as they were, had the potential to go much higher for 1940. The company pointed out that sales in the fourth quarter represented 34 percent of total sales for the year, a strong indication the Champion was building momentum. In addition, Studebaker had signed nearly 1,000 new dealers, greatly broadening the company's market representation. The implication of all this, of course, was that 1940 would be a much better year for Studebaker.

But other events were taking place that same year, and some of them affected Studebaker directly. War had broken out in Europe, and the French government placed a much-publicized order for 2,000 trucks. Bill Knudsen, director general of the Office of Production Management, the government agency charged with overseeing America's defense production program, asked automakers to cut back on the use of certain critical metals, including zinc, nickel, and aluminum.

Although America was not yet part of the fighting, Britain and France desperately needed more planes, trucks, and guns. They turned to America, with its mighty industrial base and vast supply of capital, labor, and materials. Knudsen, former president of General Motors, was using

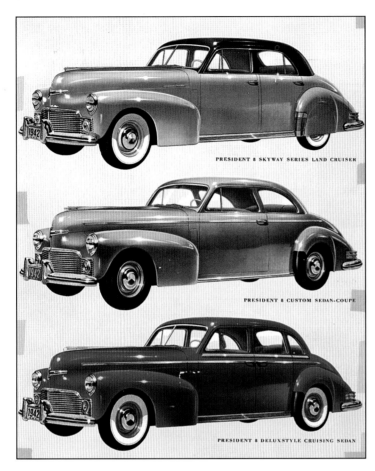

PRESIDENT 8 SKYWAY SERIES LAND CRUISER

PRESIDENT 8 CUSTOM SEDAN-COUPE

PRESIDENT 8 DELUXSTYLE CRUISING SEDAN

The lovely lines of Studebaker's President series for 1942 are
readily apparent in this picture. The Presidents were big,
handsome machines, well trimmed and powerful.

all of his considerable powers of persuasion to encourage the automobile companies to bid on defense orders. Automakers responded, bidding on work and having plant space retooled to produce war materiel.

Despite the high promise indicated in 1939, Studebaker's business results were only moderately better in 1940. Sales of passenger cars and commercial vehicles increased by about 5,000 units for the year, well under what company executives had hoped. Dollar volume was up, too, though only modestly. Some very good news was that the Earned Surplus account grew to $4.3 million, all of which had been earned in the two most recent years.

During the fall of 1940, amid mounting tensions about material shortages, production cutbacks, and growing worries that America might be dragged into the war, Studebaker introduced its 1941 product line. Champions were restyled to give them a look more in line with the

senior cars. The 1941 Champion lineup offered a range of models, including three-passenger and five-passenger coupes, a two-door Club Sedan, and a four-door Cruising Sedan, all in either Custom, Custom Deluxe, or Delux-Tone trim.

The Commander could be had in coupe, Cruising Sedan, or Land Cruiser sedan in either Custom or Skyway trim, or you could get the Cruising Sedan and Land Cruiser in Delux-Tone trim. The most desirable Studebaker was the President series on a 124.5-inch wheelbase, offered in Custom or Delux-Tone Cruising Sedan and Land Cruiser models, or those same two plus a coupe in the Skyway trim.

Each line had its own engine: a 169.6-cid in-line six-cylinder for the Champion, a 226.2-cid six for the Commander, and a 250.4-cid straight eight for the President. It was a well-balanced lineup of good-looking automobiles with roomy and comfortable sedans and stylish and sporty coupes. Styling details like low-set grilles that stretched across the front, prow-like hoods, and stylish use of exterior brightwork ranked these among the better-looking cars the company had produced.

In addition to the business of building and selling cars, Studebaker bid on military orders and won some significant contracts. By early January 1941, the company had agreements to produce high-powered aircraft engines on a cost-plus basis. Three plants were equipped for the job: South Bend, Fort Wayne, Indiana, and Chicago. The company also designed several military trucks and received an initial order.

Sales of cars, trucks, and military products were up for 1941. Especially gratifying were car sales, solid proof Studebaker was on its way to becoming a larger automaker. During fiscal 1941, Studebaker sold a total of 133,855 passenger cars, commercial vehicles, and military trucks, up 12 percent from the 119,509 sold in 1940. Dollar volume shot up 37.5 percent to $115,700,333. After taxes, a net profit of $2.4 million was recorded. The Earned Surplus balance rose to $6.7 million. The once-broke company now had more than $15 million in cash, a fairly substantial sum for that era.

In the fall of 1941, Studebaker introduced its new 1942 cars and trucks. The Champion, Commander, and President series returned with detail changes and improvements. Champion offered a range of models, including a three-passenger coupe, five-passenger "double-dater" coupe, Club Sedan, and four-door Cruising Sedan, all in either Custom or Deluxstyle trim. The Commander and President offered a range of coupes and sedans in Custom, Deluxstyle, and Skyway trim. Grilles

This advertisement covers all the bases. The central theme is the new Studebaker lineup for 1942: the President 8, Commander, and Champion. Also mentioned is the new Turbo-matic drive, a fluid drive transmission. At the top of the ad are Flying Fortresses powered by Studebaker-built engines and at the bottom are the famed Studebaker heavy-duty military trucks.

were more elegant, trim was refined, and all in all, these were very handsome cars indeed.

Given the company's renewed strength and momentum in the marketplace, along with its highly popular automobiles, there's every reason to believe 1942 would have seen another jump in Studebaker's sales volume and

position in the industry. Until the very last weeks of 1941, the outlook for the company's automobile business was for a steady increase in sales and market share. But in December, the whole world was turned upside down, and all the plans that Studebaker and every other automaker had made went out the window. The war that everyone hoped America could avoid had come.

At Pearl Harbor, Hawaii, American sailors were tending to their assigned jobs, while others were resting below deck. Suddenly a vast armada of Japanese warplanes appeared in the skies overhead. Their mission: destroy the Americans in a vile sneak attack. Since Japan had declared no war, they caught the Americans off-guard. In a hellish maelstrom of smoke and fire thousands of young men lost their lives. Sheer murder is all it was. Though Japan won the battle, it brought them nothing but dishonor.

So America was at war. With the onset of hostilities, the need for military production increased exponentially. Automobile production was officially suspended as of January 31, 1942, per government order. Studebaker reported to its stockholders that its major contribution to the war effort would be the manufacture of heavy-duty military trucks and aircraft engines. The company was already producing the trucks, but with the onset of war the production rate was increased substantially. The company also noted that since no retooling for car production could be expected for the duration of the war, it anticipated that when hostilities ended, Studebaker and all other automakers would resume production with the current models. For the rest of the war years, Studebaker occupied itself with war production. The company would amass a proud record.

Studebaker's total dollar volume of business for 1942 was the largest for any year to that point. Net sales came to $221 million, a whopping 91 percent increase. Patriotically, Studebaker refused to get rich off of war work; its profit for the year was a mere $2 million, less than it had made in 1941 despite the huge increase in volume.

One particularly important contract called for the production of Wright Cyclone aircraft engines, used on the mighty Flying Fortress long-range bombers. The airplane engine production and increased volume of heavy trucks meant the company had to greatly increase its work force. The Studebaker employee count nearly doubled to 20,000 men and women.

In 1943, Studebaker's dollar volume again broke all records. Sales were an incredible $364 million, a 64 percent increase over the 1942 record. Profits, after setting aside $1.5 million in a special Reserve for Contingencies, were a modest $2.8 million. Working capital increased to

COMMANDER CUSTOM CRUISING SEDAN

COMMANDER SKYWAY SERIES SEDAN-COUPE

COMMANDER DELUXSTYLE LAND CRUISER

Studebaker sales of the 1942 Commander series were on the upswing, and if it hadn't been for World War II interrupting its progress and upsetting the marketplace, the company might still be here today.

Reserve for War Contract Termination Contingencies and Postwar Reconversion. On February 23, 1945, directors declared a dividend of 25 cents per share. Studebaker didn't have a policy in place to pay fixed dividends on a regular basis but paid them from time to time depending on its financial position.

By now the company was allowed to brag about a previously secret project, a small tracked vehicle it developed and was producing, dubbed the Weasel. A personnel and supply carrier designed to travel "over the severest kinds of terrain . . . through snow, mud, sand, swamp [and] deep water," the Weasel could go places even a mule would avoid.

The war finally ended in 1945 and Studebaker, like other companies, was faced with the task of converting its production back to civilian products. It was a daunting job that called for essentially a complete tear-up, since none of the wartime products had civilian applications. As tough as the heavy Studebaker trucks were, there would be little demand for them in the civilian market, and whatever demand there was would be met by war surplus vehicles. Likewise, the Weasel was too costly and limited in purpose for practical civilian use. The company could continue to produce them for military use, but the Army already had more than it needed. In any event, Studebaker was eager to return to the automobile market. At its core, its heart, the company was an automaker. The company had been advancing before the war and was anxious to get back on track.

In May 1945, the aviation engine contract was terminated, and in August 1945 the contracts for military trucks and Weasels were likewise terminated. Management reported that the company's plants were converted and ready to begin production of civilian passenger cars and trucks on October 1, 1945. Unfortunately, strikes in supplier plants prevented full-scale production from getting underway, and only an insignificant number of

$22 million, and the company had more than $26 million in cash on hand, though much was in the form of advances that were restricted to use in performing war contracts. In February 1943, the Board of Directors declared a dividend of 25 cents per share, the first dividends shareholders had seen since 1932. The company boasted it had built more than 30,000 aircraft engines and more than 100,000 trucks.

For 1944, Studebaker's sales volume increased again, up 14 percent to a nearly unbelievable $415.7 million. Studebaker's output of war materiel to date was in excess of $1 billion. The company's products were helping win the war on virtually all fronts. A huge fleet of Studebaker trucks was the backbone of the Red Army's substantial field transportation system, serving a mighty force hell-bent on annihilating the German Army. Company profits rose to $4 million for the year, after a $1.5 million addition to the

This advertisement placed just eight months after Japan's murderous sneak attack boasts that Studebaker, America's oldest builder of highway transportation, was producing Wright airplane engines for the mighty Boeing Flying Fortress heavy bomber.

vehicles were built by December 31, 1945. It was a lost opportunity that came at a critical time, a sign of the times perhaps but also a bad omen.

During the war Studebaker produced more than 63,000 Flying Fortress engines and 197,678 heavy trucks for the Allied armed forces. The last war product Studebaker built for World War II was a Weasel delivered in August 1945. Dollar volume fell substantially for 1945, which was not unexpected. Sales were $212.8 million, a little over half the prior year's figure. However, a tidy profit of $3.2 million was reported. At year-end, working capital stood at $33 million.

Automobile production wouldn't begin in any meaningful way until January 2, 1946, when it resumed on a limited basis. Production was hampered by strikes at supplier plants and among suppliers of raw materials. The problems, though extremely distressing, were by no means limited to Studebaker. Strike fever was rampant throughout

As in every American military action since the Civil War, Studebaker stepped in to provide the equipment the army needed. The Weasel tracked personnel and cargo carrier was just one of the special products Studebaker supplied to the war effort.

nearly every industry. It was a difficult time for American business and certainly not a shining moment in the American labor movement. The attitude among workers didn't bode well for the future.

The company put its best face forward. Hoffman and Vance declared that "Studebaker resumes its position in the transportation industry with that position greatly strengthened and improved. Studebaker is stronger financially; it is stronger in organization; and particularly it is stronger in public regard because of its accomplishments during the war."

The company had survived many things: the transition from horses to motor vehicles, the black pit of the Great Depression, bankruptcy, and the deadliest war in history. Although it didn't realize it, Studebaker now would face its greatest challenge: the postwar era of hard and brutal competition, of great rewards tempered by great risks. The war was over; it was time now to get back to the business of making and selling automobiles.

New 1946 Studebaker Champions come off the assembly lines. The company was late getting back into production and initially offered only the low-priced Skyway Champion series. The man behind the wheel of the car on the left reportedly is Bill Studebaker, a family member and company paymaster.

CHAPTER FOUR

1946-1952
The Fabulous New Studebaker

lthough World War II ended with the surrender of Japan in August 1945, the Studebaker Corporation didn't resume automobile production in a significant way until January 2, 1946. Management explained that there was nothing wanting in Studebaker's factories or manufacturing processes to hold it back. The problem was simply the strike mentality which had infected American workers of that era.

Everywhere men were laying down their tools and walking picket lines, striking for higher wages, more benefits, and fewer hours. At times it seemed an effort to instantly redress any wrong, real or imagined, that ever existed between labor and management. In the process, it harmed companies both large and small. Naturally, it hurt the smaller firms worse. In any ranking of manufacturing companies in America in 1946, Studebaker would have to be considered quite a large firm, but in the rarified atmosphere of the auto industry, it was still a small company. Unfortunately, the strikes wounded it sorely.

Although these labor problems were not unique to Studebaker, the result was that in the race to return to volume production of passenger cars, Studebaker was very much an also-ran. It remained stuck at the gate as the remaining months of 1945 played out. Ford, Nash, and Hudson all

managed to resume car production faster than Studebaker. Other companies suffered labor problems yet, somehow, they managed to produce cars.

The importance of making a speedy return to automaking was not simply a matter of corporate pride. Getting a fast start on auto production was important to capturing a leading position in the crucial postwar market. It was important to Chevrolet and Ford, and it was critical to Studebaker because the company was starting out further back in the pack. Studebaker's owner base and dealer strength were meager compared to the Big Three, and if the company hoped to join their ranks one day, it needed to get a jump on sales.

Besides, the auto market just then was a rich orchard ripe for picking. Everyone knew that demand for automobiles would be enormous in the postwar years. Because no automobiles had been produced since January 1942, America's automobile fleet was wearing out. Trucks, too, were badly needed, since they'd gotten hard use during the war years, hauling supplies to plants throughout the country. No trucks had been produced during the war to replace the thousands of vehicles that worked on farms, and for factories and delivery firms.

For the next few years, to 1948 or 1949, manufacturers would be able to sell every car they could build without resorting to discounts or

This good-looking sedan is a 1946 Studebaker Skyway Champion. The most popular model in the Studebaker line, it carried a suggested price of $1,097. Production of the 1946 models came to less than 20,000 cars before the company switched over to the all-new 1947 models.

price-cutting, and without spending large sums of money on advertising. Buyers were lined up, ready to purchase just about anything with wheels. Millions of Americans yearned for a new car and had plenty of cash from working double shifts at defense plants. All an automaker had to do was to produce as many cars as possible. Profits would be enormous; the situation was practically a license to print money. One has to wonder why Studebaker's managers were not able to accomplish what other firms had done: get back into serious production before the end of 1945.

When production did finally resume in South Bend, the cars that rolled off the lines were basically warmed-over 1942 models. There certainly was nothing wrong in that, since every other company was returning to market with a warmed-over prewar car. The public didn't mind. They needed wheels now and after all, a new car was a new car.

Yet the 1946 Studebakers were not exact copies of the 1942s; they had new features and a few modest styling updates to change the look a

1947 Studebaker Champion Regal De Luxe 4-door Sedan for 6 passengers. This body style also available in the Commander model.

1947 Studebaker Commander Regal De Luxe Coupe for 5 passengers. This body style also available in the Champion model.

1947 Studebaker Champion Regal De Luxe 2-door Sedan for 6 passengers. This body style also available in the Commander model.

Dramatically different, and daringly postwar, the 1947 Studebakers were the first all-new cars from a traditional U.S. producer. They caught the nation's attention and proved extremely popular.

It was originally embraced as an inexpensive way to expand representation during the industry's early years, but in the hotly contested postwar market it was viewed as costly and inefficient. Eliminating distributors meant eliminating a middleman, boosting the corporation's margin. Eventually, all the U.S. automakers abandoned the distributor system, though remnants exist even today. In certain parts of the country, sales of Toyota and Subaru vehicles are handled by distributors.

Studebaker chose to produce only Champion models for 1946, which were renamed the Skyway Champion. In all likelihood, management thought that concentrating on its low-priced series would focus attention on products that in the coming years would be competing in the largest volume segment. However, in view of market conditions and considering Studebaker's product plans for the next five years, it was not the wisest decision.

The fact is the company could easily have sold every 1946 car it produced regardless of price range, and for the sake of profitability it would have been sounder to build only Commanders and Presidents, or at least a high percentage of them in addition to the Champion. After all, the company planned to assemble its prewar models for only a short time, so it made

bit. The changes to moldings and trim were enough to distinguish the 1946 cars from the pre-war models.

The company decided in August 1944 to end its relationship with its distributors, the independent firms in charge of distributing cars to entire areas of the country. The use of distributors was a common practice in the prewar period and managed to last even into the postwar era. Within their territories, distributors maintained their own dealer network and controlled sales and distribution, parceling out automobiles to dealers and taking a small mark-up on each car.

sense to maximize profits. In any event, only Skyway Champions were built for 1946, with production limited to less than 20,000 units. Then the line shut down for new model changeover. Studebaker was about to spring a tremendous surprise on the industry: a new automobile that would electrify the public.

Management called 1946 "a year of decision." The company reported a profit for the year of just under $1 million, a surprisingly good figure in view of production lost to material shortages and the cost of tooling up for 1947 models. However, digging deeper into

The lineup of all-new 1947 Studebakers included this sharp Champion Regal Deluxe three-passenger coupe. This attractive car carried a base price of just $1,451, an exceptional value in the low-price field.

the numbers one sees that the company actually suffered an operating loss of $8.1 million, offset by the application of carry-back tax credits of $10.5 million. After deducting for federal and Canadian taxes, Studebaker was left with its profit—small, but better than a loss. But the profit hadn't come from building automobiles; it was a refund of past taxes. Regardless, by midyear the company was operating on a profitable basis and expected to continue to do so. During 1946, the company declared two 25-cent dividends despite the small profit for the year.

A large part of the operating loss for 1946 was the cost of tooling new products, acquiring additional facilities, and replacing worn equipment—more than $13 million. There was a simple but exciting reason why tooling costs were so high.

While most U.S. automakers were happily turning out prewar models to be quickly snapped up by an eagerly accepting public, Studebaker was about to make an important product move. Before the close of the war, management boldly decided that the company would be the first to introduce a genuine postwar car: an all-new design that would be years

With its limousine-style coach doors, this four-door sedan offered styling and excitement like no other 1947 car. Although production was ramped up strongly, it couldn't keep pace with demand.

ahead of everything else on the road. Vance and Hoffman said their decision was based on "the conviction that the company stood to gain much from being the first to give its customers the advantage of advancements both in design and production methods accumulated during the war and which, in total, represented substantial progress."

Since it was believed that several companies planned to introduce all-new cars for 1948, it was crucial for Studebaker to move before then. The company wanted the new car ready for introduction as a 1947 model by the fall of 1946, or sooner if possible. The company had to work fast to meet the deadline.

It was worth the effort. There are probably not enough words to adequately describe how extraordinarily impressive the 1947 Studebaker was. When it arrived in mid-1946 it seemed to be something from the future, a light-year advancement. The new Studebakers boasted wider, envelope-style bodies, devoid of separate front fender shapes and with only a hint of a separate rear fender. Rooflines were flatter and sleeker, and front ends featured low, neatly integrated grilles. The look was as modern as tomorrow and excitingly "postwar."

(Above) For 1947 Studebaker boasted one of the best-looking convertibles on the market. If material shortages hadn't held back production, the company could have sold many more of these beauties.

(Left) Staff designers in the Studebaker Styling Department discuss the placement for a Champion nameplate in this posed photo.

The public practically swooned at the sight of the remarkable cars. People who'd never in their lives visited a Studebaker showroom were standing in line to get a glimpse. The dramatic new Studebakers convinced many long-time Big Three buyers to become Studebaker owners, which of course was the whole point of being first to introduce an all-new car.

Initially, the design was to be done by Loewy Associates, the prestigious independent design house headed by the flamboyant French industrial designer Raymond Loewy. Studebaker retained Loewy as a styling consultant, and some considered him the maestro of Studebaker's styling efforts. But Roy Cole, engineering vice president, disliked Loewy. Cole managed to convince one of Loewy's designers, Virgil Exner, to work secretly on a competing design. Cole arranged for Loewy's men to get design parameters calling for a much narrower car than the company wanted. Exner, working on the real parameters, was able to trump the Loewy design. However, Exner's design drew heavily on the Loewy team's efforts so the production car is generally attributed to both parties, though at the time it looked like Exner was the genius behind it. Naturally, Loewy was furious about Exner's disloyalty and fired him immediately. Exner went to work for Studebaker.

The new cars debuted in spring 1946 as early 1947 models. There were two series, Champion (the Skyway part of the name was dropped) and Commander. Champions rode a 112-inch wheelbase, up 2 inches from before, and for power had an 80-horsepower 169.6-cid flathead six. Commanders rode a 119-inch wheelbase, just as in 1942, and were powered by Studebaker's trusty 226-cid six-cylinder, good for 94 horsepower. Prices were up substantially from 1946, which in turn were up sharply from 1942. Champion prices ran from a low of $1,378 for a stripped three-passenger coupe up to $1,902 for a Regal Deluxe convertible. Commanders were priced from $1,661 to $2,236. That wasn't a problem, though; postwar inflation was forcing everyone to raise prices, and a lack of competitive pressure would keep prices high for the time being.

The most exciting and controversial of the new Studebakers were the five-passenger coupes, which featured a radical multi-pane rear window that wrapped around, giving more rear glass area than had been seen before and causing wags to pose the amusing question: "Which way is it going?" Regardless of the jokes, the look was dramatic and arresting. Nothing like it had ever been seen before. Plainly, Studebaker had grabbed the mantle of America's Styling Leader.

The 1947 models rocketed Studebaker to the forefront of public awareness. Management stated, "It is quite evident from the public's reaction to the 1947 Studebaker . . . that this decision will prove to have been one of the most significant in the company's history."

The decision to introduce a new car in mid-1946 rather than a year or two later has been controversial for many years. There are those who feel the company wasted millions of dollars introducing an all-new design long before it was needed. They hold that Studebaker could have continued selling its prewar cars through 1948, putting off the vast new tooling expenditure until then and greatly enhancing corporate profits.

There's nothing inherently incorrect in that belief. Hudson held off redesigning its cars until 1948 while Nash waited until 1949, and it didn't seem to have much adverse affect on them. The market leaders also held off as long as they could. Ford, for example, didn't introduce a new car until 1949. But Vance and Hoffman's point about the advantages of getting the jump on the Big Three is a valid one. Perhaps it's best to view the decision in light of the companies' comparative standings in the industry and what they hoped to accomplish.

Nash and Hudson were smaller automotive firms than Studebaker. In Hudson's case, the long-range plan was simply to sell more cars. Like Studebaker, Nash wanted to grow its business by taking more share. The company planned to enter the lowest price field as soon as the supply of raw materials and components could support the move. But Nash planned a gradual expansion, growing its business steadily over the coming decade rather than trying to rush it into the space of a few short years. Nash believed it was more prudent to expand and improve its dealer network first, carefully building it up to handle greater volume. Studebaker was already in the low-priced field, and its planning involved rapid expansion in a much shorter time. Management hoped to increase sales volume as quickly as possible, pushing the company into the ranks of the biggest producers. It was an aggressive strategy, and like most such strategies, it involved a certain amount of risk.

The second part of the company's postwar program was to boost production to take advantage of opportunities to increase sales. During

1948 Studebaker Champion Regal De Luxe 4-door Sedan for 6 passengers. This body style also available in the Commander model.

1948 Studebaker Commander Regal De Luxe Convertible for 5 passengers. This body style also available in the Champion model.

1948 Studebaker Champion Regal De Luxe 2-door Sedan for 6 passengers. This body style also available in the Commander model.

the year, Studebaker purchased a plant in Canada in which to assemble cars and trucks and also added materially to its existing plants in the United States. As a result of the additions, which Studebaker completed in 1946, the company could boast the ability to produce more than twice as many vehicles as in 1941. Alas, by the end of 1946 that capacity was yet to be tested, for in fact the company built fewer cars in 1946 than its prewar levels.

On the plus side, truck production for 1946 was four times that of Studebaker's best prewar year and by early 1947 was running higher than even 1946's outstanding rate. For 1946, the company reported production of 120,763 cars and trucks. Studebaker had stolen a march on the big boys; now it had to make the most of its head start.

There weren't many styling changes to the 1948 Studebakers. Naturally, with the most modern lines in the industry and production unable to keep up with demand, there was little need for changes.

Production of the 1947 models continued throughout most of the 1947 calendar year, which in light of the early introduction meant a greatly extended model year. There was an even greater emphasis on trucks this year. The company's commercial vehicle lineup now ranged from light-duty pickups to heavy-duty line haulers. Studebaker truck models covered about 90 percent of the truck market. Since the war, the company had become a major truck producer, which was another part of its efforts to become a major automaker.

The company reported production of 67,811 trucks during 1947, up 56.9 percent from the 43,196 produced in 1946. By year-end, truck production was traveling at a rate of 80,000 units, six times higher than the company's best prewar year. An invigorated Studebaker was advancing in all areas.

Things were working to plan as Studebaker outperformed the auto market as a whole. The company produced 191,451 cars and trucks, exceeding the prior year by 58.5 percent and setting a new record. In fact, during the year the company broke all its previous daily, weekly, and monthly production records, and the final quarter was the best three-month period in company history. Dollar volume rose to $268 million, an amazing 89 percent increase, and net profit climbed to $9 million, the best ever to that point. However, the company noted that sum represented a less than 3.5 percent return on sales. Management blamed the low profit margin on the high price of steel and iron, which were both still in critically short supply. That was certainly an issue, but there were other, unspoken reasons why the cost of producing automobiles had risen so much.

The truth was the company had a burgeoning problem with its labor policies. While the rest of the country was still struggling with labor unrest, enduring strikes in an effort to keep labor costs in line, Studebaker had chosen to bow down to union demands rather than risk losing momentum in the marketplace.

Equally bad was the low productivity, which was a direct result of Studebaker's inability to properly manage its plants. For decades the company had prided itself on being a good place to work, a

One of the most memorable designs created by Studebaker was the lovely Starlight coupe. Its unique wraparound rear glass caused many wags to ask the question, "Which way is it going?"

"friendly factory." For years, workers had responded by giving a day's work for a day's pay. But now things were slipping; work standards were said to be among the lowest in the industry. The result was rapidly escalated production costs.

Competitor Nash-Kelvinator, for example, produced 115,914 vehicles for 1947—some 75,515 fewer than Studebaker—yet reported a profit of $18 million. Of course, Nash also produced appliances through its Kelvinator division, but the facts show Nash's profit was double what Studebaker's was on total sales of $250 million. This was about $18 million less than Studebaker's.

The problems could be partially hidden by the large sales increases—after all, a $9 million profit was still rather substantial back then—but only for a while. Like other automakers, Studebaker was able to price its cars higher because of exceptionally strong demand in the market. But the clock was slowly ticking away: once postwar production caught up with demand, there would be pressure on automakers to reduce prices to stay competitive. In that atmosphere, a reduction in labor costs, either through increased productivity or reduced pay, would be necessary or the whole company might unravel. A day of reckoning was approaching, but it was still far off in the misty future,

Cantrell of New York was still producing Studebaker station wagon bodies in 1949. This fairly expensive unit would probably have been produced for a resort hotel or a gentleman's country estate.

and for all anyone knew, it might never come. For now things could go on as they were.

During 1947, management arranged to buy the government-owned plant in South Bend where the company had produced airplane engines. The plant, for which Studebaker paid $3.59 million, contained nearly a million square feet of floor space the company wanted to use for its growing truck business. To supplement its steel supplies, the company also acquired the Empire Steel Corporation of Mansfield, Ohio, for $7.4 million cash. At year-end, Studebaker as a whole had a net worth of $48 million. Management expressed its belief that 1948 would be an even better year.

At the dawn of 1948, a network of 11 plants outside the United States stood ready and waiting to produce Studebaker cars and trucks for world markets as soon as sufficient materials became available.

During the year a new plant in Hamilton, Ontario, began operations, producing cars for Canadian and other Sterling markets.

In the United States, production of the 1948 Studebakers got underway in November 1947. The cars were mostly unchanged—since they were already the most modern cars on the road, there was little need to update them—though the line now introduced convertibles in both the Champion and Commander series. In design studios, Loewy stylists mocked up several station wagon designs, but management chose not to produce them. The station wagon market historically was small because the expense of the wooden bodies limited demand, but it was an area where growth was possible with the right product. Willys had already shown the way, introducing the first all-steel family station wagon on the market, and was enjoying good success.

Seeming to be a completely new car, the 1950 Studebaker was in actuality a facelift of the previous model. The ultra-modern styling—reminiscent of a space ship or jet—proved extremely popular for a while.

In April 1948, President Truman appointed Paul G. Hoffman head of the Economic Cooperation Administration. Hoffman resigned from Studebaker, and no one was elevated to replace him. Chairman Harold S. Vance now added the job of president to his other duties. Although other automotive leaders had similar responsibilities, it called for a well-rounded person with both sales and production experience. Hoffman and Vance had been an ideal team; operating by himself may have overtaxed Vance's abilities.

In 1948, success smiled once more upon Studebaker. Vance was able to report the greatest year in Studebaker's 96-year history. The company produced 233,457 cars and trucks, a 22 percent increase over the record set in 1947. Dollar volume set a new peacetime record of $383.6 million, beaten only by 1944 when Studebaker's plants were going all out with war production. In addition to the stunning 43 percent

increase in sales, the company recorded net profits of $19 million— more than double the 1947 results. It was proof of the old industry adage that the greatest profits are found in volume production. The company paid dividends of $1.75 per share, a reasonable amount in light of the excellent profitability. Management said the dramatic increase in profits was entirely due to the outstanding sales volumes. The break-even point (the number of car sales needed to break even) was about the same as in 1940. The continuing increase in car sales was fueling the big profits. Management expressed a hope that continuing shortages of steel and iron would be eliminated in 1949, at which point they could produce even more cars and trucks.

Truck sales grew only marginally during the year, a consequence, the company said, of downtime resulting from production being shifted

Among the best-looking trucks of the 1950s were the Studebaker 2R series vehicles. This sharp 1950 model shows clean, modern lines and a roomy cab. *Photo courtesy Mike Mueller*

to the new truck plant. In the spring of 1948 the company introduced new truck models. They were modern designs, the best-looking trucks the company had ever produced, fully competitive with Ford and Chevrolet.

There were signs at the end of 1948 that the supply of automobiles was finally beginning to catch up with demand, though basic demand remained strong. Studebaker expected to continue to reap great sales, as did every other automaker.

Production of the 1949 Studebakers began in January. Grilles were restyled and bumper guards set farther apart to achieve a look

of greater width. Other changes were similarly modest. Since the cars were selling well, the company could hold off a major restyling until the following year.

In 1949, for the first time since the war, automobile production was limited only by capacity. Raw materials were in good supply. Studebaker outpaced the industry, producing a record 304,994 cars and trucks at its plants in South Bend, Hamilton, and Los Angeles. Of that total, 12,996 were produced in Canada and 33,760 in Los Angeles. Dollar volume set another new record: $473 million. The

Presenting the "next look" in cars

NEW 1950 STUDEBAKER

Success breeds success! The car that led in modern design now moves still more spectacularly out ahead!

The new 1950 Studebaker is here—and you can see at a glance that it's America's "next look" in cars.

Here's the dramatic and unexpected sequel to the tremendously popular "new look" in cars that Studebaker originated three years ago.

Here's a truly inspired 1950 Studebaker—dynamically new in form and substance—America's most advanced new car—styled ahead and engineered ahead for years to come.

Paced by a breath-taking new Studebaker Champion in the low-price field, this is a complete line of completely new 1950 Studebakers.

Each one is increased in wheelbase length and over all length—thrill-packed with the new performance of higher compression power —comfort-cushioned with self-stabilizing new Studebaker coil springs.

Discriminating America is giving the 1950 Studebaker an enthusiastic welcome. Stop in at a nearby Studebaker showroom the first chance you have. See the 1950 Studebaker —the "next look" in cars!

©1949, The Studebaker Corporation, South Bend 27, Indiana, U. S. A.

Studebaker bragged that its futuristic-styled cars featured the "Next Look." The Studebaker cars had boldly different styling, making Studebaker the style leader this year.

profit margin showed encouraging improvement, 5.83 percent versus 4.98 percent the year before.

A large part of that improvement came about when Studebaker was able to stop using conversion steel—nonautomotive steel in ingot form that is sent to another mill where it's rolled and converted into automotive-type steel. Certain types of conversion steel had to be sent to a third facility for further processing. Many firms used conversion steel during the early postwar years, since it was a necessary though costly short-term solution to the steel shortage. Now with steel in plentiful supply, Studebaker sold its Empire Steel subsidiary, losing nearly $1 million on the sale but netting cash that could be used elsewhere. Steel prices were much lower, which boosted the company's margins.

At the end of 1949, Studebaker had $40 million in cash, $14 million in government bonds, and a net worth of $85 million. This

The clean lines, bold frontal styling, and envelope body of this 1950 Studebaker Champion Regal Deluxe four-door sedan made it a standout among low-priced cars.

For 1950 the Commander seemed the fulfillment of the public's dreams of ultra-modern transportation in the exciting postwar era. No one had any trouble identifying a Studebaker on the road.

The blind quarter on this Champion Deluxe three-passenger coupe gives it a custom look that is very sporty. Cars like this had strong appeal to younger buyers.

Once again Studebaker offered standout styling, which it described as "The next look in cars." Though controversial, the new Studebakers were very popular.

from a company many people once thought was ready for the boneyard.

There was one dark cloud, however. Management told stockholders that the upward trend in profit margins was about to reverse. The company had scheduled a 30 percent increase in first-quarter car and truck production, to the highest level in company history, and to strengthen its competitive position was reducing prices on all models by $82 to $135. In many ways it was a smart move; the market was becoming more competitive, and lowering prices was a valid strategy to grow volume. Still, the almost cavalier way in which management spoke of reduced profit margins seemed odd.

For 1950, Studebaker introduced what was probably its most controversial design ever. Design work was handled by Loewy employee Bob Bourke, who said Loewy told him to make the Studebaker "look like zee airplane." The basic body shell was retained, but the front end was given a complete and radical redesign featuring rounded front fenders flanking a central bullet-nose shape, with twin grilles set low in a deeply undercut area just below the spinner nose. To many, it was the look of the future, a car Buck Rogers might drive. To others it just looked bizarre. It was divisive, people either loved it or hated it, but no one could ignore it or mistake it for another car. In the end, it was a tremendously successful product, and the company was justifiably proud of it.

The Studebaker Land Cruiser was the biggest Studebaker for 1950. Riding a long 124-inch wheelbase, it was base-priced at $2,187.

Popular with people who preferred a sporty coupe over a big family sedan, this Champion Regal Deluxe five-passenger Starlight coupe offered great styling and economy at a price of just $1,671.

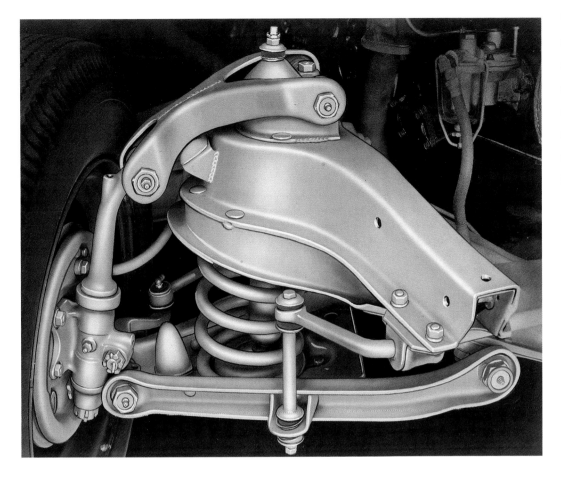

This detail of the new front suspension in the 1950 Champion shows the shock absorber mounted within the coil spring. Note the rubber-mounted stabilizer bar, which is attached to the frame and to both lower control arms.

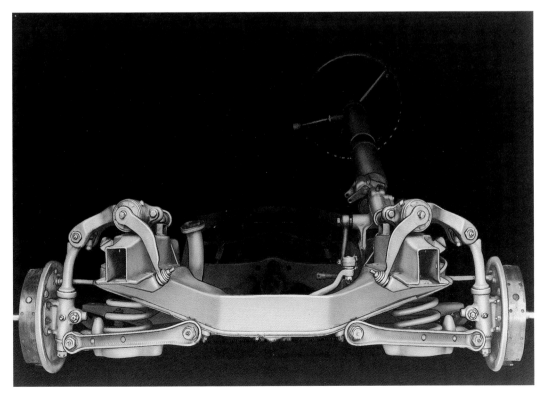

Here's a full view of the new independent front suspension for 1950. The rugged front end included rubber insulation at the top and bottom of each spring for smoother, quieter operation.

More than most companies, Studebaker took pride in its employees. Advertisements like this one touted "father-and-son craftsmanship." "These craftsmen come largely from a community where Studebaker has been in business for 99 years" it stated, calling its workers "solid citizens keenly aware of their responsibility to the public for maintaining the generations-old Studebaker standards of quality."

Public response was good, and at year-end the company reported that during 1950 it produced 334,554 cars and trucks, up 9.7 percent, a slowdown in the rate of growth but an increase nonetheless. Dollar sales rose just 1 percent, however, and net profits were $22.5 million, yielding a profit margin of 4.72 percent. Management said the decline in net profits was due primarily to higher taxes and a substantial loss in production during the fourth quarter because of "labor difficulties incident to the establishment of work standards on the new 1951 model." And, of course, prices were lower.

Also troubling was the fact that although profits dropped by $5 million, the company chose to increase dividends by more than $2 million. One has to wonder what the rationale was behind that.

Studebaker added lower-priced Champion Custom models at the bottom of its 1955 lineup. Prices on these budget-friendly cars were very

Studebaker craftsmen Glen and Harold G. Basey are known as "electricians first class"—a father-and-son team of tool maintenance experts.

Studebaker father-and-son craftsmanship helps to reduce repair bills

As most car mechanics will tell you, a Studebaker seldom needs serious repairs if it's treated half-way right.

Men with deep-rooted pride in good work build wear-resisting stamina into every detail of a Studebaker's structure.

These craftsmen come largely from the community where Studebaker has been in business for 99 years.

They're solid citizens keenly aware of their responsibility to the public for maintaining the generations-old Studebaker

standards of quality. Impressive numbers of them are members of father-and-son teams.

If you want to get more mileage out of your car—and out of today's dollars as well—decide to do your driving in a gas-saving, repair-saving Studebaker.

You can purchase one that's exactly suited to your needs at a surprisingly low price.

STUDEBAKER
Builder of trustworthy cars and trucks
© 1951 The Studebaker Corporation, South Bend 27, Indiana, U. S. A.

The year 1951 was important for Studebaker because it was the year the company introduced its new V-8 engine. Styling revisions were made to the front end, with a new grille and revised spinner.

Studebaker put a strong advertising push behind its new V-8 for 1951. Champion, meanwhile, was dubbed "The Top Value of the Top 4 Lowest Price cars." This Commander V-8 sedan is a particularly attractive machine.

good: the Champion Custom two-door sedan was priced at just $1,487, the four-door sedan at $1,519. Though Ford and Chevy prices were a bit lower, Studebaker was in the ballpark.

More than $13 million went to plant improvements and new tooling. The biggest expenditure was tooling for a new V-8 engine for 1951. In this, Studebaker was well ahead of the field. Mighty Packard, one of the greatest names in the luxury car field, wouldn't have a V-8 until 1955. Nash wouldn't produce its own V-8 until mid-1956, though both Nash and Hudson would offer the Packard V-8 in 1955. Even Pontiac wouldn't field a V-8 until 1955. Ford had long offered a V-8, and Oldsmobile had one, too, but Studebaker matched them now, which was important because V-8s were what the public wanted. V-8 demand would grow by leaps and bounds in a short span.

The Studebaker V-8 was well engineered, displacing 232.6 cubic inches and developing 120 horsepower. It was designed for future

"A brand new high-efficiency V8" says the sales brochure for 1951. Studebaker's V-8 trumped the other independents. Even luxury car builder Packard wouldn't offer one until 1955.

increases in displacement, but to keep it as light as possible there was a limit on how great an increase could be handled. That wasn't viewed as a problem, since many engineers believed future horsepower increases would rely on increased compression ratios more than raw cubic inches, and that probably influenced the design of the Studebaker V-8. Regardless, it was a worthy engine and an important product feature.

In 1950, forces were at work that would greatly influence the auto business. War had broken out on the Korean Peninsula, and the United States was drawn into the conflict. Initially, the situation stimulated demand for new cars; perhaps the public worried about not being able to buy a car if it continued very long. In any event, industry production set a new record in 1950, with 8.3 million cars and trucks produced.

By year end, however, materials were in short supply because of demand for military products. This exerted a downward pull on car production, though military production partially offset the drop in sales volume. During the year, Studebaker received important contracts for military products, chiefly heavy-duty trucks and aircraft engines. Meanwhile, the company also continued to expand production capacity by adding an eastern assembly plant in New Brunswick, New Jersey.

The 1951 Studebakers were unveiled in October 1950. The Commander series was powered by the new V-8 engine, while Champion made do with the 85-horsepower six. Cost shaving saddled the Commander with a shorter wheelbase than before. Both series now shared a 115-inch wheelbase.

Studebaker corporate performance for 1951 can be viewed in different ways. On one hand, the company recorded its highest dollar volume in history—$503,308,865.88, breaking the half billion–dollar mark for the first time—while working capital and net worth both showed improvement. But profits sank to $12 million, a drop of nearly $10 million, mainly because government price controls meant

cost increases on raw materials were only partly recovered. In addition, productivity failed to show any substantial improvement. GM and Chrysler had taken costly strikes to get labor costs in line, while Studebaker had caved in to union demands. The cost of doing so was starting to show up. The company's profit margin for the year was just 2.51 percent, down from 4.72 percent. Dividends of $3 per share were equal to 56 percent of earnings, whereas in 1950, they'd been 35 percent of earnings. The financial figures were very troubling but were shrugged off as a bad year caused by extraordinary circumstances. Everything would be okay once things got back to normal. Or so they thought.

In 1951, military production accounted for about 12 percent of Studebaker's total sales. The company estimated that would rise in 1952 to nearly 50 percent. For the first time in memory, the annual

The sale of accessories grew in the postwar era as an affluent public showed an increasing desire for luxury and custom equipment in the cars they bought. Here are a few of the many accessories Studebaker offered.

STUDEBAKER CUSTOMIZED ACCESSORIES AVAILABLE AT EXTRA COST

Automatic tuning Stratoline radio! Studebaker's Stratoline radio is just like a costly home console in performance, power and reliability. Exclusive noise-suppression system.

Deluxstyle bumper guards! These eye-arresting guards combine rugged construction and smart Studebaker styling into an exclusive, integrated design that blends beautifully.

Directional signal equipment! Extra safety, comfort and convenience. For left turns, move lever backward and left front and rear lamps flash intermittently—for right turns, move lever forward.

Chromium wheel covers replace standard hub caps and envelop the entire wheel with dash and sparkle, enhancing the exterior appointments.

Automatic electric clocks! Precision-made Studebaker electric clocks provide the convenience of accurate time whenever you drive. Entirely automatic, clocks are soundly engineered.

Sunsure Deluxtex seat covers! Deluxtex covers incorporate smooth matting fibre, luxurious leatherette paneling, flat bindings and custom fit.

Stratoline windshield visor! Here's welcome protection against the sun's rays in summer—cooler riding! It also serves to keep snow and sleet off windshield in winter—reduces glare!

Studebaker celebrated 100 years in business in 1952. This year the company introduced new Starliner hardtops to the line. The gorgeous car shown here is the 1952 Commander Starliner hardtop with two-tone paint.

report failed to mention how many cars and trucks were produced that year. The total was 285,888 units, almost 49,000 fewer than 1950. If that level continued it would be difficult to justify having four automotive assembly plants, though at the moment the New Jersey plant was devoted to military production.

The following year was rich with history and profound significance for Studebaker, marking 100 years in business. The 1952 Studebaker cars were treated to yet another facelift of the existing body shell. The work was handled by Loewy's men and was a successful blending of existing lines and a preview of styling themes that would be seen on the next all-new

Studebaker. The overall design might best be termed a mix of European sleekness with American size. Front-end styling was completely revised with a sloping hood, teardrop headlamp bezels, and a more conventional low-set grille featuring a central v-theme. The new styling blended in well with the existing body, and the 1952 Studebakers were very handsome automobiles.

On February 16, 1952, the same day on which Henry and Clem Studebaker founded their blacksmith shop 100 years earlier, the company launched a year-long celebration of that anniversary. A lot had occurred since then. There was much to be proud of, along with some lessons that, it was hoped, had been learned.

Although Studebaker didn't introduce all-new cars for its 100th birthday, it did a thorough facelift of its existing cars. The result was this attractive front-end design, which helped to visually lower the car. Notice how the design theme is similar to the all-new cars that would be introduced for 1953.

Financial numbers again showed mixed results. The company's dollar volume for the year was $586 million, rising 16 percent over 1951 and setting a new record. Net income was $14.2 million, a 13 percent hike. Naturally both figures were the sort a CEO hopes to see in a celebratory year like 1952. But within the annual report were other numbers that were disturbing. The profit, while up, was nowhere near the levels reached in 1948, 1949, or 1950, in spite of the much greater sales volume. Therefore, the company's profit margin was lower. In spite of the more competitive environment, the company paid out dividends representing 50 percent of earnings. Production fell to 231,837 units, down more than 50,000 from the prior year.

In its defense, the company explained that car production was under government control, the entire industry was down, and Studebaker's drop was in line with the rest, all valid points. But the corporation was still being hampered by high labor costs and low productivity, and that most certainly was affecting profits. Even when auto production was on the rise, Studebaker had earned a large portion of its profits from defense orders. Now, with auto production dropping, it was time to get a handle on the labor situation and quickly. Although Vance and the men and women of Studebaker had no way of knowing it, a reckoning was coming. In the next two years, Studebaker would be pushed to the wall.

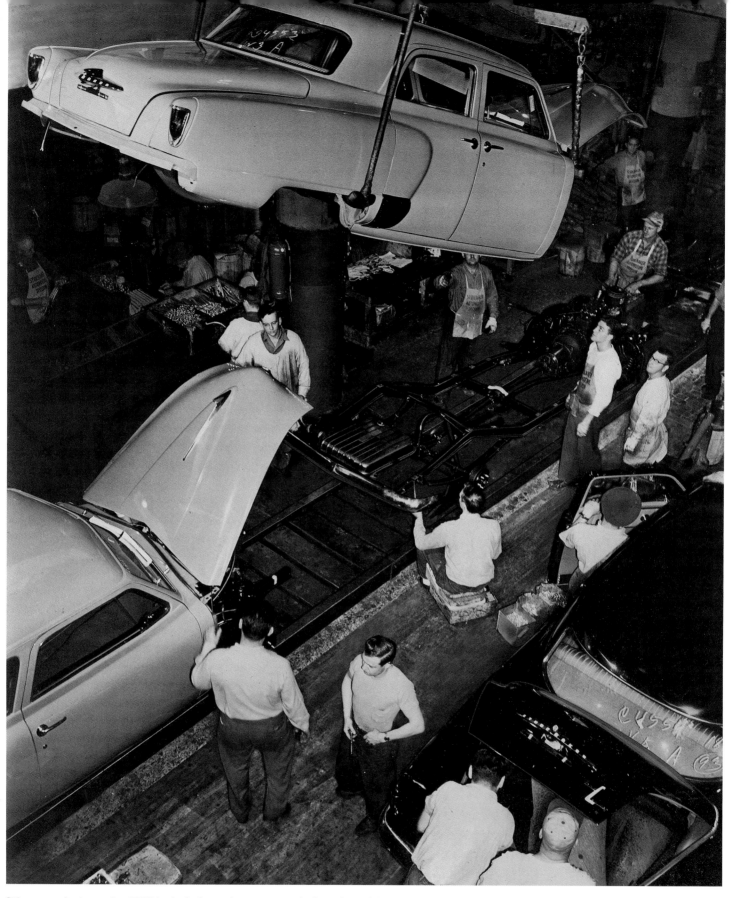

Other new features for 1952 included new bumpers, redesigned trunk lid handles, and taillights. Gravel pads on the Land Cruiser, State Commander, convertible, and Starliner were a new design. Shown is the assembly line during 1952.

The redesigned frontal appearance was a successful updating of the now six-year-old Studebaker body. This attractive Commander V-8 Starliner hardtop is shown with optional whitewall tires, chrome wheel discs, and tinted glass.

An artist's rendition of the radically new Studebaker coupe shows the dramatic styling and beauty of these landmark automobiles.

With the new Starlight coupe and Starliner hardtop, Studebaker solidified its growing image as a styling leader.

CHAPTER FIVE

1953-1958
The Fatal Errors

Studebaker had made its share of mistakes throughout its many years of business, but it was during 1953 to 1955 that the company committed the fatal errors that in time would force it to abandon the automobile business.

The sad truth is that much of the progress made by Studebaker management and employees, from the craftsmen who built carriages and wagons to those who produced military products for World War II and the beautiful postwar cars, went down the drain one year after the company celebrated its 100th anniversary. That so much could go wrong so quickly was unprecedented. Studebaker suffered a virtual perfect storm of problems.

The year 1953 was a bad time to make mistakes. In prior years, especially 1945 to 1950, errors were overshadowed by the red-hot tempo of auto sales, when customer expectations were low, profit margins high, and the industry couldn't produce enough new cars. Things were markedly different in 1953.

For one thing, the last vestiges of postwar demand came to an abrupt end. Automakers had predicted that pent-up demand would be met sometime between 1948 and 1950, but the expected slowdown was delayed by the situation in Korea. Concerns about a new war propped up auto sales from 1950 to 1952 and may have lulled automakers into thinking the frantic pace would go on indefinitely. However, in mid-1953, supply would finally catch up with demand, and when it did problems turned into crises. It was no time for errors.

Yet errors were a big part of Studebaker's story in 1953, and products were, too. The company hadn't fielded an all-new car in time for its 100-year anniversary in 1952. Rival Nash celebrated its 50th anniversary in 1952 by introducing all-new Ambassador and Statesman models and an all-new Nash-Healey sports car. In South Bend, Studebaker labored to get a new design ready for 1953.

While a talented crew of stylists were busy designing all-new '53 Studebaker sedans and hardtops, Loewy designer Bob Bourke was working up an alternative: a low-slung coupe with European styling. Bourke hoped to create a special design that might be produced as a one-off concept car for display around the country at auto shows, attracting attention to Studebaker products.

This was the age of the so-called "Car of the Future," where the Big Three showcased their design talent by creating special show cars. These were often outlandish, with wild new features and daringly futuristic styling. But something inside Bourke told him to keep his specialty

Raymond Loewy, probably the best-known automotive stylist in the world back then, stands outside as Studebaker Chairman Harold S. Vance admires the new Studebaker for 1953 from behind the wheel.

coupe grounded in reality, designed with production in mind in the hope that it might actually be produced.

Loewy followed Bourke's progress and liked what he saw. The coupe was long, low, and sleek. Based on a 120-inch Land Cruiser's wheelbase, the clean lines were breathtaking. Loewy decided to push for putting the coupe in production, reasoning it would practically sell itself. In meetings with Studebaker management, Loewy forcefully promoted the daring coupe.

It wasn't a difficult battle. Even a conservative like Harold Vance could see the advantages. The coupe cost no more to produce than an ordinary car, but its tremendous appeal would make it an easy sell. Hoffman loved the coupe's styling. Since the end of the war, management had come to think of Studebaker as a leader in styling. After all, the first all-new postwar cars came from Studebaker, and they had sparked a dramatic sales increase. The bullet-nose cars were daringly futuristic. Great styling was seen as a kind of trump card, a product advantage for Studebaker, and the new coupe would be a further demonstration of the company's design leadership. The decision was

made to put Bourke's stunning design into production for 1953. Loewy insisted no major changes be made, a smart move because it preserved the purity of line and graceful shape that was so beautiful to behold.

But the new car had been designed essentially as a single model, a two-door in either hardtop or pillared coupe versions. Bourke had put forth no companion sedan or station wagon designs. The idea was that this car would be an addition to the lineup. Someone suggested redesigning the new sedans to incorporate styling elements of the Loewy/Bourke coupes, and that's where the troubles began.

On the surface, the idea of restyling the sedans, the design of which by then was almost finalized, was good. Maintaining a family resemblance among products would help build awareness among buyers, which in turn would help sell more cars. General Motors' cars within each brand had a familial look, and even across the range of brands the company maintained a distinct "GM Look." Chrysler products of that era likewise maintained a family resemblance across the line.

Where Studebaker erred was in how it adapted the coupe styling to the sedans. The coupe's low, clean front-end and sloping rear didn't

From the angle shown in this artist's drawing, the European styling of the new Studebaker sedans has a clean, pleasing look.

Commander V-8 Starliner hard-top. White sidewalls, chrome wheel discs—and glare-reducing tinted glass—optional in all models at extra cost.   Actual color photograph.

Only Studebaker has this dramatic styling

The low-swung European look! The coming thing in car design! Enjoy it now! Nine body styles! All down to earth in price!

You saw the way all automobile designing was influenced by the original postwar Studebaker.

Now you are seeing history repeat itself. The spectacular new 1953 Studebaker has swung upon the scene—the first American car with real foreign-car distinction.

This, unquestionably, is the next "new look" in cars. This low silhouette is the coming thing in motoring.

But you don't have to wait. The excitingly different 1953 Studebaker is here now. Order yours right away—a smart new sedan, coupe or hard-top—a Champion in the lowest price field or a brilliantly powered Commander V-8.

The ultra-luxurious Studebaker Commander V-8 Land Cruiser sedan. All Studebakers offer Automatic Drive or Overdrive at extra cost.

New 1953 Studebaker

translate well when applied to two- and four-door sedans. The sedan's styling was therefore much less appealing, though apparently management liked it. Making matters worse was that all sedans, with the exception of the Commander Land Cruiser, were built on a 116.5-inch wheelbase rather than the coupe/Land Cruiser's 120.5-inch wheelbase. While the shorter wheelbase was competitive with GM and Ford products in raw specifications, appearance-wise the Euro-styling made the Studebaker's look smaller and even a bit stubby. The 116.5-inch wheelbase just didn't provide the proper sleekness. The design called for a longer chassis.

Here's the real deal: the all-new and tremendously appealing Studebaker hardtop for 1953. The styling was so advanced that at first many people assumed they were only "concept cars," something that might be produced in the future.

The pity is that this situation might have been avoided if the company had built all Commanders on the Land Cruiser wheelbase. Studebaker stylists mocked up full-size clay styling models using a longer wheelbase and flatter roofline, and they were quite handsome designs. Why they were rejected in favor of the short-wheelbase cars is unknown, but it was probably an effort to reduce costs. Saddled with the highest labor costs in the industry and reluctant to confront its union over the issue, the company had to cut corners elsewhere. A 116.5-inch wheelbase Champion could be justified since it was marketed as an economical family car, but a pricier car like the Commander called for a longer wheelbase. The extra length produced a more important-looking car.

Another problem was a time shortage. The company had put a great deal of effort into designing the original sedans, then had to revamp them with the Euro look, and the rush may not have allowed enough time to consider the choices. Whatever the reason was—and it may have been a combination of these—the decision was made and the designs went on to the next step: production. That's where the next problem showed up.

Because the low-slung coupes were so different from the taller, upright sedans, most of the body panels and trim were not interchangeable. In essence, Studebaker would be introducing two completely different cars for 1953. As a result, the company was forced to spend much more than usual for tooling. Since tooling prices had risen dramatically in the post-war era, Studebaker's cost for tools and dies for the two different car lines proved a major expense. It appears that some corners were cut and a few shortcuts were taken in an effort to rein in the rapidly mounting costs. Some of these came back to haunt the company. In addition, the complexity of trying to schedule production of two dissimilar cars on two distinct wheelbases and five different body types simply overwhelmed Studebaker's production planners.

Initially, it looked like the company had scored another major coup. Studebaker dealers and the car-buying public fell in love with the new Starlight hardtops and Starliner coupes. And why not? They were the best-looking cars on the road. In fact, they still rank among the best-styled cars of all time. Available in six-cylinder Champion and V-8 Commander series, they represented a bold stroke, with Studebaker once again snatching the role of styling leader from mighty GM. Orders flowed in from an ecstatic dealer network

Then disaster struck. When the first cars came down the assembly line, a major glitch appeared: the front-end sheet metal wouldn't mate to the body. Something had gone wrong somewhere with die-checking

The breathtakingly beautiful 1954 Studebaker Starliner hardtop was the style leader of 1953 and 1954. Today this fine automobile is recognized as one of the most beautiful cars of all time.

procedures or pre-production testing. It may have been the result of shortcuts taken to cut costs or it may have been something that was simply unavoidable, but whatever the cause, the effect was immediate. Production ground to a halt. Die changes were required, which took time and cost a great deal of money, and production was set back by weeks. New car introduction didn't come until January 1953.

Apparently Studebaker's production system was simply overwhelmed by the task of introducing two separate lines of cars in one year. A better plan would have been to introduce the coupes and hardtops—the glamour stars of the day—in 1952. This would have made them available in time for the 100th anniversary celebration, and they could have been built alongside face-lifted 1952 sedans. The following year, restyled sedans could be introduced. If introductions had been stretched out in this manner, the people in charge of product decisions might have had time to improve their appearance.

It took a while to straighten out the tooling mess-up, and it wasn't long before the next problem cropped up. The sales division had underestimated the selling appeal of the coupe models, so initially the company didn't produce anywhere near enough cars to meet demand. Perversely, they also seriously overestimated demand for the awkward-looking sedans. Apparently, the sales planners based their projections on prior year model breakouts, without taking into account the vastly greater appeal of the new Starlight and Starliner. In the end,

two-door sedan production fell by nearly 50 percent, four-door sedans by 30 percent, while production of coupes more than doubled, and hardtops were up 20 percent. The sad thing is the company could have sold many more coupes if production had gone smoother and forecasts had been closer to demand.

All the snafus called into question the company's abilities, and for good reason. The list of problems was much lengthier than it should have been. And more would be added.

Talk to people who bought a new Studebaker in 1953 and there's a good chance you'll hear comments about the poor quality of the cars. To put it bluntly, build quality wasn't up to the relatively lax industry standards of that decade, and it certainly wasn't up to the proud standards set by generations of Studebaker workers. The problem seems to have been a combination of poor workmanship and some substandard parts purchased as cost savings.

In one well-documented instance, an engineer authorized substitution of a proven door lock mechanism with one that cost 10 cents less per car. The latch was cheaper, but it soon created problems when car doors began flying open on sharp turns. The company eventually fixed the problem, but it was a black mark against the product and cost a fair amount to correct.

The failure of workers to put more effort into building a better car was inexcusable. For years they'd been paid high wages in the belief that

Paul G. Hoffman and Harold Vance pose with the new 1954 Conestoga wagon. The two executives had saved Studebaker in the 1930s when the company was in receivership, but some historians feel that by 1954 Studebaker should have replaced them with younger, more aggressive leaders.

in return they'd work hard and maintain quality. Yet in truth, many workers began to goof off once they met the day's piece-rate quota. To fill the remaining hours in their workday they'd play cards, take a nap, or read a newspaper. In effect, they were working part-time but getting full-time money. Meanwhile, the company's problems began to snowball.

Studebaker lost money on car production during the first quarter of 1953. It wasn't until April that profitability was reached. In May, the factory was forced to cut production sharply when workers at transmission supplier Warner Gear went on strike. The final stroke of bad luck, the *coup de grace*, came in the fall, when Henry Ford II launched what became known as the Ford Blitz.

Ford wanted to regain sales leadership from Chevrolet and announced he'd outsell them or kill the company trying. Ford factories began producing thousands of extra cars that were shipped to dealers (unordered in many cases), leaving retailers no choice but to sell them or go bust. It created a fire sale mentality, with Ford dealers selling cars for a few dollars over invoice, sometimes at a loss, and even selling new cars as slightly used on used car lots. Anything and everything was done to move the metal, and it worked, as Ford sales climbed rapidly. Chevrolet had no choice but to follow suit, and the two biggest auto divisions in the world became locked in a battle for supremacy. Meanwhile, Chrysler

and the independent brands saw their sales fall off the charts in the last quarter of the year.

The effect on Studebaker's business results was apparent. Dollar volume for 1953 rose slightly to $595 million, about $9 million more than 1952, but net profit fell more than 80 percent to $2.68 million, and none of it came from auto production. Current assets fell by more than 25 percent, working capital dropped by more than $3 million, and the company's net worth was some $4.3 million less than before. Yet, and this is bewildering in light of the company's history, dividends were higher than the previous year! Such a sharp reversal in earnings called for fiscal restraint; it was time for circling the wagons, not holding a party. Certainly Vance and Hoffman could recall that they'd been elevated to their current positions precisely because Albert Erskine had insisted on paying generous dividends despite falling profits. Why this was allowed after such a damaging year is difficult to understand. Had no one learned what could happen?

In the 1953 annual report, Vance and Hoffman detailed the difficulties the company faced and talked about what they called the "demoralization of the retail market" caused by harsh sales practices, reduced sales, and low profit margins. They noted that this demoralization had carried over into 1954, an understatement if ever there was

The 1954 Champion four-door sedan. When looked at by themselves it's a little harder to fault the styling of the new sedans; however, their sleek lines tended to make them look smaller than competitors' cars and narrower, too.

The new Studebaker Commander station wagon for 1954 revived the legendary Conestoga name. Although not unattractive, the new Studebaker wagons were unfortunately offered only in two-door models, while the automobile market was quickly moving to the new four-doors introduced by competitors.

Stylists made sure the interior trim of the new Studebakers was also stylish and exciting, as seen in this Studebaker interior shot.

industry sales of 60 million new cars between 1954 and 1964 and noted that even given Studebaker's relatively small percentage of the market, that total would ensure a large and prosperous business for the company and its dealers. It sounded almost as if they thought the company could sit back and abundant sales would simply fall into its lap, with the other auto companies ceding Studebaker its rightful share. Could they have really been that naive?

If management really believed things were going to be easier in 1954, their hopes were quickly shattered. As difficult as 1953 was, 1954 would prove to be a vast deal harder. The Ford Blitz continued into the new year even more intensely. Sales of Hudson, Nash, Packard, Kaiser, Willys, and Studebaker cars fell to their lowest levels in years. None of the independents were profitable. In fact, for America's independent makers, 1954 was a turning point, the year when the final consolidation of independent companies would begin.

one. The two leaders then declared that relief would come only when "all car manufacturers have adjusted their factory production to the level of what their dealers can sell on a profitable basis." Apparently it didn't occur to them that the Big Three were more interested in selling as many cars as they could than they were in protecting another manufacturer's profit margin.

Hoffman and Vance further stated that the long-term outlook was encouraging because the auto market was growing. They projected

Although the 1953 and 1954 sedans have had their share of criticism, the longer wheelbase of the Land Cruiser models went a long way toward improving the lines.

Studebaker didn't have much that was new in its product lines for 1954. Coupes and sedans were carried over with minor trim changes and mechanical improvements. The biggest product news was the introduction of the all-new Conestoga station wagon. Getting into the station wagon market was a welcome move because wagons were among the hottest products that decade. However, the company was late getting there. Willys had put the first all-steel wagon into production in 1946, and Nash launched its popular Rambler wagon in 1950. Studebaker was among the last volume sellers to bring out a wagon.

To make matters worse, the Conestoga was a two-door at a time when the market was rapidly turning to four-door wagons. Not only were the four-doors more popular, they commanded much higher prices. The same year Studebaker unveiled its two-door wagon, Nash unveiled a new four-door Rambler wagon on a longer wheelbase, and it became a huge success.

As if all this was not enough, the problem of labor costs was coming to a head because Studebaker's rapidly deteriorating financial situation meant the problems could no longer be swept under

the rug. The company had avoided a labor confrontation in prior years by caving in to demands and tacitly accepting mediocre work standards and low productivity. The result was that workers came to view high pay and easy work as a basic entitlement. For a time, management convinced itself that its car's high quality and superior styling compensated for the higher prices. Hoffman, who'd returned to Studebaker to try to fix the labor problem, had once declared that Studebaker had "the friendliest factory in America," but that was merely papering over an inability to deal with the union. Refusing to face a growing cost problem is poor management regardless of how it's packaged.

If Hoffman believed the union would now voluntarily chip in and work harder for less money, that utopian dream existed in his mind and nowhere else. Instead, both company and workers went through weeks of hard negotiating before reaching a compromise that still wouldn't be enough to completely solve the problem.

Around this time, someone suggested a merger might solve a lot of problems. The idea had come up more than once since the end of the war, but Vance always resisted; he wanted Studebaker to

The 1954 Commander Starlight V-8 coupe was simply stunning in this red-and-white two-tone combination. The wide whitewall tires were a popular touch. Owner: Ron Wakefield.

Looking at the clean, low lines of this 1954 Commander Starlight it's easy to see why these cars are so highly sought after today. Owner: Ron Wakefield.

1954 Studebaker Regal Land Cruiser V-8 for 6 passengers

Here's another view of the Studebaker Commander Regal Land Cruiser V-8 for 1954. This was a large, well-trimmed automobile for anyone desiring a powerful and luxurious family car.

remain an independent. At the end of 1953, Vance predicted the situation would turn around and the company would soon be in good shape again.

But he was wrong. Sales were awful, and Studebaker continued to bleed. Events soon reached a crisis stage. Model year production for 1954 was half the 1953 pace, which hadn't been very good. To put it in perspective, during 1950 the company reported factory sales of 334,554 cars and trucks. In 1954 factory sales were, at just 113,920 cars and trucks, about one-third of that. A 66 percent drop in sales would cripple the strongest company, and Studebaker was by no means the strongest. And, of course, profit margins had been higher on the 1950 cars.

In the first quarter of 1954, the company lost $8.3 million and was running out of cash. The large amount of money paid out in dividends,

The 2R series trucks that Studebaker produced between 1949 and 1953 were among the best-looking pickups of the 1950s and proved very popular with customers. This scene shows the new trucks nearing the end of the assembly line.

or to fix tooling problems, and used to pay excessive wages meant there was much less to prop up the company until business turned around. By April, Studebaker had no alternative but to merge.

Choosing a company with which to merge was fairly simple. Willys-Overland and Kaiser Motors had already merged in 1953, and neither had enough money to prop up Studebaker, so joining with them was not an option.

Nash and Hudson were due to merge in May 1954. In the 1940s, Nash CEO George Mason talked with Vance about putting Studebaker, Nash, Hudson, and Packard together, but Vance rebuffed him. Mason had since decided Studebaker wouldn't work out as a merger partner after all, since the company had the highest labor costs in the industry and a strong, militant union. Studebaker's close ties to South Bend would make it difficult to move production to another state, which might be necessary to reduce costs. Nash and Hudson were both based in Detroit, and their cars were close in size and could easily share a common body.

That left Packard, which had approached Vance in 1953 about a merger only to be rebuffed. But now, facing disaster, Vance was more willing to talk. In many ways, Packard seemed an ideal partner. Although the company was currently struggling, overall Packard was sound. The two companies' products didn't compete with each other; Studebaker sold in the lower price ranges while Packard was a longtime and well-respected producer of luxury and medium-price cars. Best of all, Packard still had a fair amount of cash.

Packard's president was a brash, ex–appliance executive named James Nance. Nance started out with National Cash Register before joining GM's Frigidaire division. From there he moved to General Electric's Hotpoint Appliance division, where he made a name for himself as a hotshot sales manager and executive. Under his direction, Hotpoint was propelled into the top ranks of appliance makers.

Nance had been considering the automobile business for several years. Its large size and importance appealed to his ego, and he believed his sales ability and manufacturing experience qualified him to be a strong and effective leader in the automotive field. He wasn't interested in joining any of the Big Three as a midrange executive working his way to the top. A high-level appliance executive, he was interested only in a top-level position with an automaker. Packard had intrigued Nance; it was a prestigious firm and one he could join as chief executive. He became its president in 1952.

By early 1954, Nance was also looking for a partner. For years, Packard had been coasting along, an old-line automaker with a great name that had seen better days. The company was no longer the leader in the luxury car field and was now selling mostly medium-price cars by trading on the Packard name. Lacking aggressive management or exciting products, the company was in danger of slowly fading away.

After assuming the Packard presidency, Nance worked to grow the company, bringing in new men and launching an expensive program to build new manufacturing facilities and develop new products. He spent enormous sums and in two years managed to increase car sales slightly while doubling the company's dollar volume. However, his profligate spending and inexperience in the auto business meant Packard's profits had actually fallen slightly.

Nance knew Studebaker had labor and cost issues, and he worried Vance and Hoffman would want to run the show, which would be unacceptable to him. On the plus side, Studebaker had a large dealer network and was considered the top-selling independent brand. The fact that many industry analysts felt Studebaker offered the best chance for volume sales deeply impressed Nance. He realized that if a fair number of Studebaker dealers added Packard franchises, it could greatly increase sales of his big cars. And over time, Studebaker, Packard, and Clipper cars could be redesigned around a common body shell, which would greatly reduce tooling and amortization costs for both companies. Pooling resources, eliminating duplication, sharing parts, and making joint purchases to increase buying power were some of the benefits of merging.

The financial situation was rapidly deteriorating, however. Although Packard recorded a profit of $5.4 million in 1953—down slightly from 1951 and 1952—by the time it was ready to discuss merging the company was losing money at a fearful pace. The losses began toward the end of 1953 and continued into 1954. By March, Packard financial Vice President Walter Grant warned the company was "rapidly approaching bankruptcy."

Studebaker was also running out of money and was nearing a point where it must either merge or declare insolvency. Earlier, Paul Hoffman, who'd been working only part time as Studebaker's Chairman, announced

For 1955 Studebaker introduced the exciting President Speedster. This "show-car-turned-production-car" wowed the public with its sleek lines and exceptionally well-trimmed interior.

he'd work on a full-time basis to push through a new labor contract to lower costs significantly. The fact that the chairman hadn't considered his job important enough to work full time speaks volumes about management's mindset at Studebaker. Hoffman and Vance were no longer the aggressive young executives they'd once been. They were older and perhaps overconfident. Complacency seems to have set in at all levels of the company.

After weeks of contentious and difficult talks, Hoffman and the union worked out an agreement that did away with the ruinous piecework rates in favor of a regular wage. But without the self-imposing piecework standards (lax as they were), the job of boosting productivity fell to Studebaker's foremen, who were woefully inadequate for the task. It would take a great deal of time to train them in managing people effectively and improving productivity without triggering a walkout. Meanwhile, Studebaker continued to hemorrhage cash at a sickening rate.

The company suffered another big loss in the second quarter, reportedly some $12 million. Packard, too, was losing money. Problems were closing in on all sides.

Representatives from the two firms met to iron out the merger details, and that's where the biggest mistakes were made. Merging two large companies calls for a close examination of the books, a review of the financial status of each firm with estimates of costs, and details on profits and losses. Because of the upheaval in the retail market neither Studebaker nor Packard looked very promising on paper. Both were losing money, Studebaker at a much faster rate. In all likelihood, neither side wanted to get into protracted negotiations that might drag on too long to do any good. In what happened next there's more than a hint that each side was trying to bluff or pull the wool over the eyes of the other. For its part, Studebaker was nearly broke; it had to join with a cash-rich partner soon or perish. Packard, too, was losing money and its retail sales were fading into nothingness. It needed a boost from a volume car seller whose dealers, it was hoped, could help sell Packards and Clippers. After the union of Kaiser with Willys, and Nash with Hudson, it was plain that the day of the stand-alone independent was over. Both companies needed to grab a partner quickly or perish.

Neither party looked forward to having their ledgers examined, so the decision was made that no such examination would occur. They declared it would be a friendly merger using figures put forth by each party, including estimates of break-even points. From them, Nance guessed that the combined firms would lose $9 million in 1955, post a much smaller loss for 1956, and record a handsome profit in 1957 when all-new cars debuted with a shared body. His calculations might have been correct, providing the information on Studebaker's break-even point was right and every part of his program went as hoped.

The two companies officially became one on October 1, 1954, with Paul Hoffman as chairman and James Nance as president. It was plain from the start that Nance would be the man who actually ran the firm.

The merger joined the oldest transportation company in America with one of the most revered luxury car names in the world. Together, they were the fourth largest automaker in America, a company with the potential to grow or sink depending on how it was led. The combined companies boasted more than 4,000 dealers, two lines of automobiles, a line of trucks, substantial military business, and long-standing reputations. They also had a shortage of cash, extreme financial losses, gross overstaffing, low productivity, continuing labor problems, and dismal sales. Their plants were mostly older and, in the case of Studebaker especially, not in the best condition. On average, their dealers were smaller than the Big Three and not as well financed. One fact is clear: whatever it did, the new Studebaker-Packard Corporation had to move quickly. Time was fast running out.

The actual terms of the merger were that Packard was purchasing the name and assets of Studebaker. Over the years, this has raised some eyebrows, although it's an altogether normal practice in cases of corporate mergers. Nash had bought Hudson, and Kaiser had purchased Willys; it was nothing out of the ordinary. For a few days after the merger, there were the usual round of media conferences, statements to reporters, and press releases flowing out from the company that emphasized the great advantages now held by the joint companies. But problems soon cropped up.

Nance grew worried about the continuing losses at Studebaker and sent vice president of finance Walter Grant to South Bend to get an idea of Studebaker's cost problems. While there, Grant discovered, to his horror, that Studebaker had greatly underestimated its break-even point. Instead of the 165,000 cars related in merger discussions, Grant estimated the breakeven point at 282,000 cars—more than 70 percent higher!

Nance was in a state of shock. Here was disaster in full form—rarely in its history had Studebaker exceeded that level of sales! But Hoffman rejected Grant's estimate, pointing out that Studebaker had been profitable in 1952 when production was around 230,000 units. That was true, but that profit included a large volume of military business not related to car production. In addition, in 1952 competition wasn't nearly so strong as 1954, and margins were better.

Grant's estimate was probably pessimistic, but it showed that Studebaker's costs were too high. The problem wasn't so much the rate of pay; rather, it was the low productivity. Too many workers doing too little work destroyed any chance for Studebaker to earn a profit. Until the problem could be corrected, the South Bend division was going to lose a great deal of cash and occupy a large portion of management's time. Meanwhile, the bleeding continued.

On October 8, American Motors chairman George Mason died unexpectedly after a brief illness. The day after the funeral, AMC's board of directors elevated George Romney to president, chairman of the board, and CEO. In press interviews, Romney spoke of a reciprocity agreement Mason and Nance had reached in which each side pledged to buy components and parts from the other in roughly equal dollar amounts. It was, according to the phrase used, "love without marriage." AMC was spending enormous sums buying V-8 engines and automatic transmissions from Studebaker-Packard and expected a reciprocal purchase of parts from AMC to even things out. When Romney was informed by his procurement staff that Studebaker-Packard wasn't honoring its part of the agreement, he sent a telegram to Nance suggesting they meet to discuss the situation.

Nance replied to Romney by letter, refusing to meet and denying any reciprocity agreement. Nance had made sure to add wording to the agreement giving him an out and used the excuse that AMC's prices were higher than other suppliers. That conveniently ignored that the price Studebaker-Packard was charging AMC for engines was about $200 higher per unit than if AMC built them. An outraged Romney ordered his engineers to begin work on a V-8 to replace the one AMC was buying. He stated to an executive, "We can't do business with someone who lies."

Years later, Nance told an interviewer that the reason behind Studebaker-Packard's failure was the death of Mason and the ascendancy of George Romney. According to Nance, prior to his becoming Packard president, he and Mason had fashioned a secret agreement to merge all four independent automakers.

Nance claimed that Mason told him to take over Packard and then merge it with Studebaker. Meanwhile, Mason would purchase Hudson and merge it with Nash. Once those two transactions were complete, the two surviving companies would be merged into one, and Nance would take over as CEO when Mason stepped down. Nance even claimed he would never have gotten involved with Packard or Studebaker if Mason hadn't talked him into it.

For years, this story has been accepted at face value, which is bewildering since it falls apart when examined in any sort of detail. Nance claimed Mason asked him to take over Packard so together they could merge the four firms. But in 1948, when Romney was about to join Packard as a top executive in line for the presidency, Mason talked him out of it, convincing him to go to work at Nash instead. Since this was around the time Mason first approached Packard about merging, one has to wonder why he didn't urge Romney, a friend with whom he'd worked on wartime production planning, to take over Packard, rather than ask a complete stranger like Nance, a man with no auto experience.

Romney was well versed in the industry even before he came to Nash in 1948. In the years since, Romney had learned even more because Mason was training him to assume management of the company upon Mason's retirement. Yet Nance claimed Mason was going to turn over the reins to him when the time came. For such a thing to be possible, Mason would have had to lie to Romney from 1948 to 1954 and betray him once the four-way merger was completed.

Anyone familiar with Mason's character would testify he was utterly incapable of that sort of dishonesty. One also has to wonder about Nance's intelligence and suitability as a chief executive if a complete stranger could talk him into making a life-changing career move and a disastrous merger. Nance was many things, but it's doubtful he was stupid enough to buy a company he didn't want merely because a competitor told him to.

Another serious fault in Nance's story is that no one seems to recall any secret agreement except him, and he spoke of it only years after the fact. Not a single Nash or American Motors executive questioned by the author remembered any secret agreement with Nance. Though Nance claimed he and Mason agreed to have the final merger completed before the end of November 1954, no paperwork has surfaced, nor have any reports, studies, or graphs. None of the required filings have turned up, no due diligence was undertaken, nothing concrete to support his statement. Yes, there were rumors in the industry, but such rumors had been around since 1945.

One also has to wonder why Nance spent so much time during 1952 and 1953 investigating the possibility of merging with Willys-Overland, Kaiser-Frazer, Studebaker, Hudson . . . and Nash. His notes and files include many references to Nance asking for advice and information on the possibility of merging with each of the independents. If a deal had already been worked out, why spend so much of the company's scarce capital commissioning investigative reports on the viability of merging with each of those companies? After all, Nance claimed the path was already planned.

But the most significant questions to ask are these: If Nance and Mason did indeed have an agreement to merge Studebaker-Packard with Nash-Kelvinator, why did Mason approach Packard in 1954 regarding a merger of Hudson, Packard, and Nash, without Studebaker? Why was he forced to appear hat in hand before Nance and his lieutenants to plead his case for merging Packard and Nash if a deal already existed?

Nash's effort to merge with Packard has been documented by men who were involved. In January 1954, Mason made a formal presentation to Packard urging a merger of Nash, Packard, and Hudson. Mason had large visual charts created to illustrate his plan. According to someone involved in preparing the presentation, Mason was listed to be CEO, with George Romney as executive vice president, next in line of succession. Apparently Nance was to be vice president of the Packard Division. Mason's offer to merge reportedly was approved in principle by all three companies. However, in the end the Packard board was persuaded to reject the deal by none other than James Nance.

Why would he do that unless there was no secret deal? Nance had a greatly overestimated belief in his ability as an automotive executive. The number three spot at the number four automaker was a position he simply could not accept. Instead, he decided to merge Packard with Studebaker, where at least he would be top man. As one of Nance's

Another President Speedster, this restored vehicle highlights the interesting two-tone color schemes seen on these rare one-year-only sporty cars.

The 1956 Studebaker President sedan was part of a series that debuted in 1955, bringing back an old and cherished name. Although utilizing the carryover body, the Studebaker line for 1956 received a major restyling that made the cars look larger, more important, and much more conventional.

consultants put it, "Mr. Nance will never consider anything except to be the top manager of any business to which he was assigned."

Romney later heard from reporters that Nance was boasting of his intention to buy American Motors soon and that Mason had only kept Romney to carry his briefcase. The criticisms stung Romney, and he developed an intense dislike for Nance.

The result of all this, of course, was that Nash and Hudson were partnered, as were Studebaker and Packard, and that was as far as it went. It was a great deal for Studebaker because once Packard owned the company it would have to cover Studebaker's losses with Packard money. Studebaker was burning through cash like a wildfire.

When Nance finally came to realize the extent of Studebaker losses he must have had deep regrets. It was his fault for not insisting on a complete audit of Studebaker's books, but the ones who would ultimately suffer were the stockholders and employees of Studebaker-Packard. The board of directors at both firms must also bear responsibility. If such complete disregard for due diligence and fiduciary responsibility were to take place in today's corporate world, it might have landed a few top executives—Nance included—in jail. One wonders why the directors allowed it to happen.

Someone once mentioned a prevailing "good old boy" mentality as the root cause, but that's hardly true. Nash and Hudson auditors went over each other's books with a fine-tooth comb, then the two presidents hammered out an agreement over several weeks of strenuous discussions. Due diligence is always the proper course in corporate buy-outs. The complete disregard for accountability and fiscal oversight was the fault of both managements and is simply unforgivable.

The situation was summed up in the best light possible in the 1954 annual report for the new Studebaker-Packard Corporation. Net sales, including Packard for 1954 and Studebaker for October–December, amounted to $222 million. The company suffered an operating loss of $41.7 million; however, tax credits reduced the loss to $26 million. On top of losses Studebaker sustained on its own between January and September, it was a disaster.

The company had a new credit agreement for $45 million and a long-term loan of $25 million. Now it needed to move quickly to merge operations together, eliminating duplication and excess personnel as rapidly as possible. Cutting costs while bringing out new products was the only hope.

Unfortunately, the 1955 Studebakers were only mildly face-lifted versions of the carryover 1954s, which first appeared in 1953. The public had already rejected the sedan's European look and had only faint interest in the Conestoga. The coupes weren't selling either, so it was obvious Loewy's idea was a mistake. The company should have rushed through a major facelift for 1955, but lacking money and distracted by so many other problems, all that was accomplished was to add a lot of chrome to the existing cars, in hopes it would attract more buyers.

A brightly chromed grille opening with a stylish inset ornament replaced the twin grilles of the '54, and a rounder hood came with it. The Land Cruiser was dropped from the Commander series because the long-wheelbase sedan was being reserved for the President series that was just debuting. The President was a smart move by Studebaker, a longer, fancier, more upscale car aimed at Studebaker loyalists looking to move up a bit. The President line included two sedans, a coupe, and a hardtop, plus a special Speedster hardtop model, all on the 120.5-inch wheelbase. But once again Studebaker was late getting to market. The company should have been offering an up-market car years earlier so

Studebaker buyers wouldn't leave the fold as their affluence grew. As it was, the company had been grooming buyers for Buick, Olds, and Chrysler. In January, new wraparound windshields were introduced, giving the cars a bit more modern appearance.

The President series offered good styling—the long wheelbase helped—and very attractive interiors. But the standout of the Studebaker line was the new Speedster, with its simulated wire wheels, bumperettes with fog lights, special badges, gorgeous instrument panel, and quilted leather and vinyl upholstery. It drew raves from the motor press.

Dollar volume picked up for 1955, the result of including Studebaker results for the full year along with improved sales. Volume totaled $480 million, but the company reported an operating loss of nearly $31 million. Tax refunds reduced it to $29.7 million, which was bad enough. This used up the last of Studebaker-Packard's tax credits.

Factory sales of cars and trucks for 1955 totaled 138,742 versus 113,920 the prior year. Although it appeared to be a fair rebound, a better description might be a dead cat bounce. With the new President series, plus restyling on the other lines, Studebaker should have done much better. The industry enjoyed its greatest year ever in 1955: AMC was up 34.7 percent, while Packard sales doubled despite horrendous production problems at its Connor Avenue plant. Clearly, Studebaker needed a new car.

Nance went into the merger thinking he could put off a complete redesign until 1957. That was stretching it because Packard's basic shell dated to 1951, and its 1955 facelift had been a year overdue. Studebaker's body dated only to 1953. Ordinarily, a redesign should have been able to wait until 1957, but the public simply wasn't buying the car. Nance might believe he could wait another year, but the market didn't agree.

Instead of launching all-new cars for 1956, Studebaker went in for a heavy facelift. This job was accomplished mainly by Vince Gardner, a ringer brought in at the last minute when Loewy's proposal was deemed too European. Gardner, a talented designer, was forced to carry over the center section but reshaped the front and rear, crafting new fenders, hood, and deck lid to make it appear larger and more mainstream. Naturally Loewy was embarrassed to be shunted aside, but his contract was coming to an end and it wasn't going to be renewed. The company had lost confidence in his ability to create cars that would sell.

In 1956 Studebaker designers restyled the former coupe and hardtop models to create the new Hawk series. Four models were offered: Flight Hawk and Power Hawk were coupes, while the Skyhawk (shown here) was a hardtop. The most expensive model in the new series was the top-of-the-line Golden Hawk. Owner: Ron Wakefield.

On the new Hawk the sloping hood was replaced by a taller one, fronted with a radiator-style grille similar to Mercedes-Benz and Lancia cars. Owner: Ron Wakefield.

Rear styling was more conventional as well. Note the Skyhawk name spelled out in script on the ribbed rear panel of this gorgeous 1956 model. Owner: Ron Wakefield.

The 1956 Studebakers were good-looking cars. Sedans and wagons got higher, blunter front-end styling that was quite attractive. There still was no four-door station wagon even though AMC was selling them like the proverbial hotcakes. The company also persisted in keeping Commanders on the shorter wheelbase. In a bizarre misreading of popular trends, Studebaker decided most President models (two-door sedan, four-door sedan, and wagon) would use the 116.5-inch wheelbase shared with Champion and Commander. Only the President Classic got the longer wheelbase.

Meanwhile, the company's six-cylinder engine was getting long in the tooth. Engineers had talked with American Motors about purchasing AMC's excellent six, but Romney torpedoed the idea. The official explanation was that AMC needed every engine it could make for a planned expansion of Rambler production for 1957. That may have been true, but by this point Romney was unwilling to deal with Nance. So even if AMC could have spared the engines, it's doubtful he would have okayed it.

In a brilliant move, Studebaker stylists reshaped the coupe and hardtop into a new series of sporty cars dubbed the Hawk. These

Here's a side view of the new 1956 President station wagon. Although President Classic sedans rode a 120.5-inch wheelbase, regular Presidents like this wagon used the 116.5-inch chassis. Owner: Dave Trask.

Another President station wagon, this one has the optional roof rack. The two-tone paint and wide white tires give this stylish car the proper look of luxury. Owner: Dave Trask.

The Hawk series gave the Lowey coupes a new lease on life. Studebaker called them "family sports cars." With room for five, they offered outstanding performance and style.

featured a taller hood and upright grille, much like a Mercedes-Benz. Although the tooling budget was modest, it greatly altered the overall style. The Hawks, marketed as "family sports cars," included a six-cylinder Flight Hawk coupe, V-8 Power Hawk coupe, and a Skyhawk V-8 hardtop. At the top of the Studebaker lineup was the awesome Golden Hawk hardtop with a 352-cid Packard V-8, tail fins, gorgeous interior, and outstanding performance. Priced at $3,061 it was, and is, one of the most desirable cars to come out of the 1950s.

Losses continued during the year, and Studebaker-Packard's troubles mounted. Military business that had propped up the company in prior years suddenly faded away. The defense department was instituting a "narrow base" supplier network, meaning fewer companies would get contracts. Studebaker-Packard lost a $420 million military jet engine contract it badly needed. Upon reviewing the enormous losses

the company was sustaining, the banks and insurance companies that financed it turned down a requested $50 million needed for new models fearing it would be throwing good money after bad.

Company stylists had designed completely new Packard, Clipper, and Studebaker cars around a common body, but without the needed funds there was no way to pay for the tooling. The program was brilliant and if the cars had been ready for 1956, they might have changed the course of history. But the financial lords no longer had confidence in Nance. A year and a half after the merger, the company still hadn't consolidated; it had two big factories, two proving grounds, two management staffs, and too much duplication.

Nance had wanted to wait until 1957 to consolidate products on a common shell, while American Motors accomplished that by the end of 1954. The result was that Studebaker-Packard was still stuck with too much overhead and high production costs. The company had only enough money to hold on to the end of summer. Jim Nance's chickens had come home to roost.

Sales for 1956 weren't good. In its annual report, the company didn't provide the customary factory sales figures, but model year production was only 85,401 cars and some 20,000 trucks, both down substantially from the prior year. This time the problem wasn't so much a rejection of the product as it was fear of buying an orphan car. Many believed the company was about to go out of business, which naturally impacted retail sales. The result was plain to see: Studebaker-Packard recorded an operating loss of $43.7 million. The company also took special charges of $28 million for estimated cancellation costs, inventory obsolescence, and other costs, plus $32 million to write down its Packard plants, which were to be liquidated.

Its ledgers drowning in red ink, the company had decided to close out the Detroit Packard operations. Although Packard enjoyed a short-lived resurgence in 1955, it was unable to sustain it. Because of problems stemming from Nance's decision to move assembly into the undersized body plant it was leasing, Packard quality and productivity had plummeted. Like Studebaker, Packard had the stench of impending doom, and buyers shunned it.

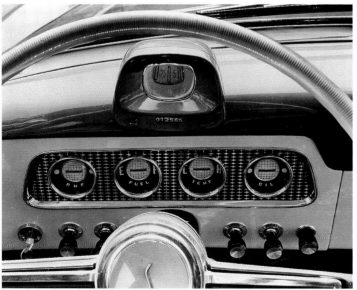

(Above) This press photo for the new Golden Hawk shows its handsome mesh grille, which would inspire the later Lark series. Notice the hood scoop, wire wheels, and fender-mounted lamps.

(Left) Studebaker instrument panel for 1956. Notice the "Cyclops Eye" speedometer was the central focal point, sitting atop the other instruments.

There were not a lot of changes in the frontal styling on the 1957 Hawk. Perhaps that's why this young lady is holding up that sign. Out back, the Hawks now had big fins and the line-up was trimmed down to just the Silver Hawk and Golden Hawk.

By midyear Studebaker-Packard was looking for a savior. Nance talked to Ford about using the Lincoln body for Packard, he also talked with Curtiss-Wright, Chrysler, International Harvester, General Dynamics, and others about merging, or selling off Studebaker-Packard's defense business; different scenarios were conceived and rejected.

In the end, only defense supplier Curtiss-Wright was interested. Its president, Roy Hurley, was mainly attracted by Studebaker-Packard's defense business and factories, such as the modern Utica, Michigan, plant where jet engines and Packard V-8s were built. Hurley realized the Eisenhower administration was anxious for someone to step in and save the

AMC also had a bad year. Its net loss was $19.7 million, but much of that was the result of spending to develop a new V-8 to replace the Studebaker-Packard unit and to pull forward the introduction of an all-new Rambler in 1956 rather than 1957, as originally planned. If Studebaker-Packard had displayed the same urgency in pulling forward new products, the financial community might have had a more favorable impression of its potential. The same institutions that refused to loan Studebaker-Packard additional money agreed to refinance AMC's long-term debt and extend credit through 1958. Although AMC was losing money, the bankers had confidence in Romney's ability to turn it around.

company. Perhaps he also thought he could save the auto business. Of course, if they merged, the company's losses would provide tax write-offs for Curtiss-Wright.

Knowing he had Studebaker-Packard over a barrel, Hurley took full advantage of it. Coyly, he toyed with Nance and the directors, first indicating he wanted to deal, then calling things off, meanwhile squeezing the Defense Department to grant Curtiss-Wright huge military orders in exchange for helping Studebaker-Packard. Hurley's tactics were cynical and mean-spirited, but they worked. Just before Studebaker-Packard was about to declare insolvency, a deal was reached with Curtiss-Wright that would save the company, for the time being.

Studebaker Golden Hawk for 1957. This year the Golden Hawk had a supercharged Studebaker 289-cid engine under the hood. Like the 1956 model, it offered 275 horsepower, but the lighter Studebaker mill made the 1957 a much better handling car. *Photo courtesy Mike Mueller*

Good-looking from any angle, the five bright chevrons and contrasting color on the fins help identify this 1957 model as a Golden Hawk. *Photo courtesy Mike Mueller*

Hurley agreed to lease the company's Utica and Chippewa plants for 12 years for an immediate payment of $25 million and paid another $10 million for the company's remaining defense business. When it came to a merger, Hurley backed off but extracted an agreement wherein Curtiss-Wright would manage Studebaker-Packard for three years at cost in exchange for an option on five million shares of stock at $5 per share. Thus, Hurley could run Studebaker-Packard as he wanted without actually taking a financial stake in the firm. If he could save it, fine; he could exercise his stock option, buy the company and use Studebaker-Packard tax credits to offset Curtiss-Wright profits. If Studebaker-Packard failed, he could shrug his shoulders, say it was inevitable, and his own company wouldn't suffer. It was a great deal for Hurley, and he'd strung Studebaker-Packard along until the company had no choice but to accept it.

The 1957 Golden Hawk's instrument panel was one of the better-looking of that decade. Note the engine-turned trim and the symmetrical placement of the instruments. In an age when most cars had only rudimentary gauges and idiot lights, the Golden Hawk stood out as a real "driver's car."

PACKARD CLIPPER . . . Four-Door Sedan

In all his time at the head of Studebaker-Packard, James Nance was never able to consolidate both brands onto a single, all-new shared body, which would have saved the company millions in development costs and production efficiencies. In 1957, with the Packard plant closed, the company cobbled together this Packard Clipper sedan on the Studebaker President body.

Part of the agreement called for Studebaker-Packard to take over North American distribution of the well-regarded Mercedes-Benz luxury cars, which would be sold through Studebaker-Packard dealers. The idea was that giving dealers another line to sell would help stabilize the dealer network while giving Studebaker-Packard another source of income.

Several times during negotiations, Hurley pointedly snubbed James Nance, angering and deeply embarrassing him. It dawned on Nance that perhaps Hurley wouldn't need his services once the deal was finalized. Like a petulant schoolboy, Nance informed the board he was leaving as soon as Curtiss-Wright took over. General Manager Harold Churchill was named to replace him.

On November 2, 1956, in what the company termed a "quasi-reorganization," Studebaker-Packard reduced the par value of its stock from $10 per share to $1 per share, using the resulting capital surplus to absorb the accumulated deficit of $48.2 million.

So 1956 marked another weary turning point for Studebaker. The Los Angeles plant was shut down, as were the Detroit Packard plants. Studebaker's New Jersey plant had already been sold. The so-called "Packard Operation" was over, and a Studebaker man was again at the top, albeit under the direction of an outside company. The corporate coffers again had money in them, so there was a chance for a future.

If Studebaker had immediately used the cash it had received to bring out all-new car lines it might have had a chance to turn things around, but Nance and his directors had spent too much time looking for help. That fall, Studebaker offered yet another revision of its unsuccessful 1953 cars, and no one should have been surprised by how the public received them.

Studebaker *Champion Scotsman* 2-Door

Full Size...Full Power...Maximum Economy

This new 2-door Champion Scotsman has everything! Crisp, clean design... full size...full power...full comfort...PLUS new three-way economy. (1) *Economy when you buy*...a price so surprisingly low...yet it includes such extra equipment as a heater/defroster, directional signals, spare wheel and tire—everything you need for safety and comfort. (2) *Economy while you drive*...up to 29 miles per gallon of gasoline with all other operating costs to match. (3) *Economy when you trade*...a proven fact based on Studebaker's historically higher resale values. For your only car...for your extra car...the Champion Scotsman is today's best value...a car that's smart to purchase, a car you can drive with pride.

Functional Interior...More Headroom...Front and Rear

This is an interior built for hard family use...style-wise beauty combined with durability. You'll appreciate its value as weeks of daily use grow into months and into years. You'll also enjoy the extra headroom built into this car, front and rear, every day you drive your Scotsman.

The new Scotsman series offered three models: two-door, four-door, and wagon. The Scotsman two-door sedan, priced at an amazingly low $1,776, was plain but attractive. Notice the windshield is framed in rubber rather than stainless steel and there are no exterior moldings. Even the hubcaps were painted rather than plated!

Studebaker *Champion Scotsman* Station Wagon

Full Size...Full Comfort...Full Utility...Maximum Economy

A full-sized station wagon at such a low initial price? Seems almost unbelievable, but it's true. The new Champion Scotsman Station Wagon is everything you ever wanted in an all-purpose car. You get the spacious comfort of a 6-passenger sedan (room for eight with optional Hideaway Rear seat)...smart, functional styling that won't go out of date in one year...full power...*plus more than 93 cubic feet of carrying space with the rear seat down.* And America's most dependable engine...the Champion Sweepstakes Six...powers the Scotsman...gives up to 29 miles per gallon operating economy. Special springing provides the support for heavy loads, yet you enjoy Studebaker's famous comfort ride when you take the family and friends for a drive. For work or play this Champion Scotsman Station Wagon is not only today's best value...it's tomorrow's too—because the traditional extra-craftsmanship built in to all Studebaker cars assures dependable low-cost service while you drive, and the lowest depreciation of all cars in its class.

Almost 8 feet long and 5 feet wide...

a total carrying space of 93 cubic feet with the rear seat and tail-gate down. Table height tail-gate for easy loading. And when the rear seat is occupied, there's still a 66 inch long space for luggage or sports equipment.

The Scotsman two-door station wagon for 1957. Color choices in the Scotsman line were limited to just three: Admiral Blue, Lombard Green, and Highland Gray. Yet despite the drab colors and plain trim, the Scotsman cars sold reasonably well and represented one of the few bright spots for Studebaker that year.

The 1957 Studebakers were mildly face-lifted. Grilles were lower and now wrapped around the body sides, giving a wider, more "important" look. The leading edge of the hood was lower, and hood fronts now boasted a stylish winged emblem. Front bumpers had a dropped center section, and new paint schemes were introduced. At long last, Studebaker added a four-door station wagon to the lineup, though for some unfathomable reason, all were produced on the 116.5-inch wheelbase. All in all, it was a decent lineup of cars. If they had appeared two years earlier, they almost certainly would have sold in much greater numbers.

The 1957 Hawk line was available as a Silver Hawk coupe with either six or eight cylinders, or as the mighty Golden Hawk hardtop, which this year came with a supercharged 289-cid, 275-horsepower Studebaker V-8 and offered vastly improved handling. Restyling was minor, though tall fins now sprouted from the rear fenders. A limited-production Golden Hawk 400 with elegant leather interior trim came at midyear.

Again this year the only President sedan on the longer wheelbase was the Classic. The Classic is easily identified by the rear door quarter window. It was a good-looking car, but the basic design, dating back to 1953, had to compete with larger, all-new cars from the Big Three.

For 1958 Studebaker introduced a new hardtop body style in the President and Commander series. This body was also shared with the 1958 Packard hardtop. The roofline was markedly different from prior Studebaker hardtops and quite stylish in appearance. However, sales of all Studebaker-Packard cars were down again this year, and the company struggled to hang on.

The 1958 Packard line included this odd-looking Packard Hawk. Based on the Studebaker Hawk, it featured a blend of details mainly seen in prior years along with new "fish-mouth" front-end styling.

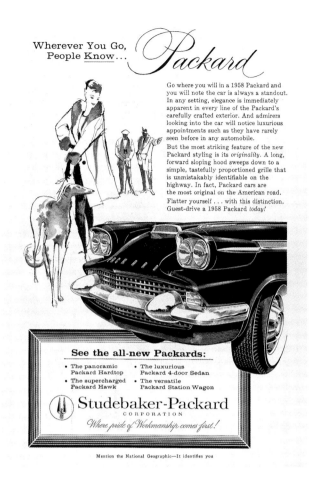

Like the Packard Hawk, the rest of the Packard line of cars was built by Studebaker in South Bend using the carryover Studebaker body. New styling on the sedans and wagons included quad headlamps. This was the final year for Packard.

With Packard's plant closed, the decision was made to produce the 1957 Packard in South Bend on the Studebaker President body. Stylist Dick Teague, who would later move to American Motors, came up with a reasonable facsimile of a Packard by applying 1956 Packard styling themes to the President. It was well trimmed and tastefully done, but most buyers saw it as just a bastardized Studebaker, and less than 5,000 were produced. However, since the tooling bill was only about $1 million, it likely was profitable for the company.

Import cars were on the rise because of their low prices and excellent gas mileage. Looking for something that would sell easily, Churchill thought a low-priced full-size car offering good mileage might attract buyers. Engineers and product planners came up with the new Studebaker Scotsman, a line of Champion-size cars

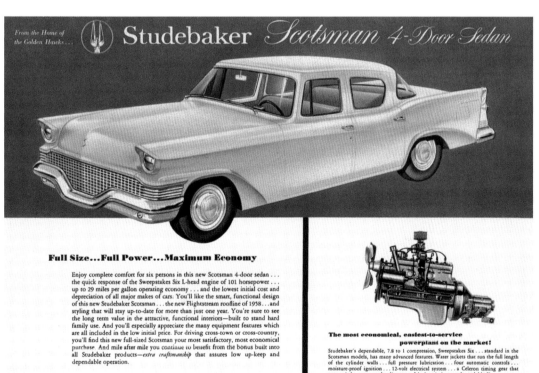

A different grille was perhaps the biggest change visible in the 1958 Scotsman cars. Five color choices were offered this year, including Glasgow Gray, Glen Green, Loch Blue, Midnight Black, and Parchment White.

Studebaker *Commander, Champion* 4-Door Sedans

When You Have Value on Your Mind

Long known for value, the names Commander and Champion take on a new deluxe meaning this year. They are (as a pleasant fact) basically low-priced cars. Yet they offer a luxury which only Studebaker could provide and still maintain quality and safety from front grille to rear fins. This pair has a wheelbase of 116.5 inches . . . length for a smooth "between-the-wheels" ride. It is length for four doors of wide convenience, length for leg room and knee room, length for a massive hood forward and a long luggage compartment aft. The exterior styling and luxury of the Commanders and Champions are evident, blocks away. But equally important are the interior features: box-section structural members to make the body a shield of steel; variable rate front springs and variable ratio steering—both for easy driving; brakes with the safest ratio of area to weight in their class, safety cone steering wheels, rubber-insulated chassis and noiseless rear axle. You start with a lot, you may add at slight extra cost Twin Traction, power steering and power brakes, Flightomatic transmission or Overdrive.

New for 1958 is the treatment of the air vents or cowls; they are now located in the grille, to leave body lines clean and sleek.

Hawk Styling distinguishes the rear fins and taillights of 1958 Commanders and Champions. New hoodline is low and wide, blending into the new roof silhouette. Dual headlights are standard on the Commander, optional on the Champion.

Studebaker *Provincial* 4-Door Station Wagon

This Low, Wide 4-Door Beauty Has V-8 Power and Pickup!

You know the moment you settle yourself comfortably behind the wheel of the roomy, sleek-looking 1958 Provincial that you've really promoted yourself to the head of the station wagon class! The clean trim line of the hood, the "four lights in a row" open-road driving protection, the eye-winning Hawk styled rear fender fins and taillights, the double safety-lock four doors, the neat and colorful Naugahyde and vinyl upholstery . . . all mark the 1958 Provincial as a standout wagon in the standout Studebaker line. Added to all its distinctive styling advances are the comfort and performance features that distinguish all Studebaker cars. There's more than ample seat room and leg room for six adults (room for eight with optional Hideaway rear seat) . . . *and more* than 93 cubic feet of carrying space when you want it. You enjoy luxury sedan comfort when you're traveling light, yet two-stage rear springs take over and prevent "bottoming" when your Provincial is fully loaded. The V-8 engine gives you that fast getaway and immediate pickup that are so important in traffic, with the kind of operating economy that you expect only from a *Studebaker V-8*. All in all, the Studebaker Provincial will make you proud you own it . . . in traffic, on the turnpike, or in the Country Club parking lot!

180 HP V-8 Engine. The Studebaker Sweepstakes 259 V-8 engine of the Provincial is in an improved short-stroke design that means less power-wasting friction. This results in noticeably increased power for starts or passing, as well as longer engine life. Fuel use is also considerably lower. Many high performance features are built in; 4-barrel carburetor, stepping horsepower up to 195, is optional.

The 1958 Commander and Champion shared the same basic body with the Scotsman, but buyers got much better trim for the extra price they paid. Commander and Champion models had tail fins, brighter colors, and nicer interiors and offered a much wider array of optional equipment.

There was no station wagon in the 1958 Champion line. Buyers wanting a Studebaker wagon had a choice of either the six-cylinder Scotsman two-door or this plush Provincial four-door powered by Studebaker's 180-horsepower, 259-cid V-8.

stripped to the bare basics. Exterior chrome was replaced by paint, even on the grille and hubcaps. It was a Plain-Jane automobile, but with prices starting at a patriotic $1,776, it couldn't help but sell. A Scotsman pickup truck was soon added.

Churchill had predicted a profit for 1957, but he was wrong. On volume of $213 million, Studebaker-Packard lost $11 million. It was a big improvement over the prior year, but it was still a significant loss, the company's fourth in a row, further eroding customer confidence.

Under the management agreement, Churchill and his executives had to follow Hurley's orders. It must have galled the old-line auto men to answer to a man with little experience and even less tact. For 1958, the company once more restyled its existing cars. Hurley declared that another mild-looking Packard like the 1957 wasn't acceptable. "People will label it a Studebaker," he told Churchill. So styling came up with a new look that incorporated quad headlamps, Dagmar bumpers, and a full-width grille. A new hardtop joined the line, as did a Packard Hawk with a fiberglass

This photo of the 1958 Studebaker President hardtop gives a better view of the grafted-on quad headlamps. The full-width grille and drop-center bumper give this car an illusion of greater width.

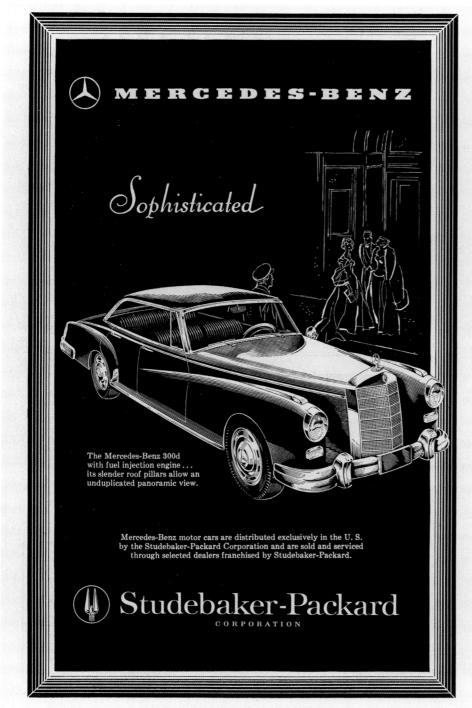

One successful pairing for Studebaker was when it began to distribute Mercedes-Benz passenger cars in the United States. Despite the relative high prices of the Mercedes cars, the Studebaker dealer network was able to make the line a success in America.

the front fenders to fit quad lamps. They were standard on Commander and President, optional on Champion. An attractive new hardtop was added to the lineup. The Scotsman returned with almost no appearance changes.

The company did its best to market its cars with the slim budget available. The entire 1958 Studebaker-Packard line was extolled in a full-color supplement placed in newspapers with a combined circulation of 16 million readers. But continual bad news about the company's financial status fed buyers' worries about purchasing an orphan, and sales continued to drop. Of course, continually restyling the same old car hadn't produced any outstanding designs either.

Studebaker's truck sales had been in a near continual decline since 1948 and by now accounted for total annual production of less than 10,000 units. Like the cars, the truck line suffered from a lack of new products and not enough money to redesign them.

nose and fish-mouth grille. The new look was certainly different, but sales tanked anyway. Apparently the buying public didn't share Hurley's beliefs. It was the final straw that killed the Packard car.

Product planners convinced themselves that Studebaker had to have quad headlamps for 1958, so stylists grafted small pods onto

Financially, Studebaker-Packard was close to catastrophe. During the first nine months of 1958, sales fell to $92 million, and the company recorded a loss of $22 million. The end seemed in sight, but Churchill had come up with a plan to introduce a new car in the hot compact market. He needed to hold Studebaker-Packard together until the car's

RARELY EVER, SUCH GLAMOUR IN AN AUTOMOBILE...

THE SCINTILLATING STUDEBAKER

Starlight

Here is a star of the first magnitude in the constellation of Studebaker-Packard
automobiles. It is the President Starlight, an entirely new hardtop of perfect proportions
crafted to high standards of workmanship and styled to standards of high fashion.

Its roof is a graceful line . . . thin, strong posts, front and rear, allow visibility that is
really panoramic. Seats and appointments are unmistakably in the luxury category.

Superior handling qualities and effortless maneuverability make the Starlight
easy to park and a pleasure to drive under all conditions.

See and guest-drive the luxurious President Starlight, or the economical
Commander Starlight at your Studebaker-Packard dealer's, *today!*

From the Home of the Golden Hawks

 Studebaker-Packard
CORPORATION

Where pride of Workmanship comes first!

Mention the National Geographic—It identifies you

One sign of the growing crisis at Studebaker-Packard is the use of mainly black-and-white advertising in 1958. The company had been one of the early pioneers of color photography for ads and now relied on black-and-white drawings, which helped disguise and smooth out the awkward styling.

introduction in the fall of 1958. A refinancing plan was worked out in which the banks and insurance companies that financed Studebaker-Packard agreed to cancel notes totaling $54.7 million in exchange for 5 percent secured notes totaling $16.5 million and 165,000 shares of $5 convertible preferred stock, par value $100 per share. The bankers would receive interest payments on the notes and preferred stock.

In giving the company some relief from its enormous debt, the bankers were gambling Churchill's new car might somehow save the business. If it did, they could convert the preferred stock to common stock and sell it at a profit. If Studebaker-Packard failed, they had notes secured by collateral, since the company had pledged virtually all of its property and plants in South Bend, plus stock in its Canadian subsidiary. Of course, in corporate liquidation, owners of preferred stock have preference over owners of common stock in the liquidation of assets—such as in bankruptcy liquidation.

The advisory management agreement with Curtis-Wright was terminated, and Hurley's option on five million shares of Studebaker-Packard stock was cancelled. Curtis-Wright agreed to relinquish its rights in the distribution of Daimler-Benz cars, and pay $2 million, in exchange for Studebaker-Packard's remaining interest in properties leased to Curtis-Wright. A new wholly owned subsidiary, Mercedes-Benz Sales Inc., was created to handle distribution in the United States. For its

(Right) We're not sure why this vehicle was produced. This is essentially a Studebaker pickup with the Packard nameplate on the hood. Some sources believe this may have been a proposal for export markets.

(Below) The 1958 Scotsman wagon offered tremendous utility at a very modest price.

part, Mercedes agreed that Studebaker-Packard wouldn't be required to pay for vehicles until they were sold or held for 150 days.

There was some good news in 1958. Sales of Mercedes-Benz cars increased. Studebaker-Packard had a military contract for 5,031 6x6 trucks, which followed a contract for 5,037 in 1957.

But of course, the big news was Churchill's new car. It was a chance to pull Studebaker back from the brink. It was a brilliant plan and it had to work; Churchill was betting the company's last dollar. Everything, including the hopes and dreams of everyone who loved Studebaker, now rested on a small car called the Lark.

Studebaker Commanders and Champions

From the Home of the Golden Hawks...

Studebaker cars take on a completely new luxury look for 1958!

1958

Studebaker President

(Left) The Studebaker cars depicted in this 1958 advertisement look a lot sleeker than the actual cars did. This artist drawing makes the headlamp pods seem to be neatly integrated into the front end, but in actuality they have a definite "added-on" look.

(Below) With scant funds to develop new products, Studebaker's truck line suffered from neglect. But as this 1958 Transtar shows, the company still made a good-looking vehicle.

THE *LARK* BY STUDEBAKER

Studebaker stunned the industry when it debuted the new Lark compact, which competed against the senior Rambler cars—the only other American-made compact. This great-looking hardtop model was the style leader of the 1959 Lark lineup.

CHAPTER SIX

1959-1961
Studebaker's Big Gamble

In mid-1957, Studebaker had reached a crossroads. The continual rehashing of the existing car, which dated to 1953, was a road that led to nowhere. Yet there wasn't enough money to develop the completely new car the company so desperately needed, nor did it look like there ever would be.

After Curtiss-Wright had finished picking the plums off the Studebaker-Packard tree, it became clear that the merger once contemplated was unlikely to ever be consummated. Roy Hurley seemed content to treat Studebaker-Packard as a personal fiefdom, running it as he saw fit without putting any cash into it, beyond the payments already made. The problem was that with Hurley disinclined to merge there appeared to be no solution to Studebaker-Packard's basic problem: poor-selling products and insufficient capital to field new ones.

Obviously, no financial institutions were willing to invest in what looked to be a dying automobile company. Harold Churchill could see the situation would force him to continue using the existing body for the foreseeable future, and if he didn't somehow create a winning product from it, Studebaker's future wouldn't be very lengthy. The outlook grew increasingly bleak.

Thus, when it came to what sort of future product direction the company should take the choices were few. The new car, whatever it was, had to be based heavily on existing tooling. The most expensive part to tool, the basic body shell (or center section) had to be retained. There wasn't any money to redesign it. There could be new front- and rear-end sheet metal and some chassis engineering, but in the end whatever resulted would have to be in essence what had gone before, altered by whatever the designers could do to rework it on a very limited budget. Churchill believed, rightly, that trying to create yet another "big" Studebaker out of what would by 1959 standards be a narrow and undersized body would only result in another sales decline. And although the company's break-even point had been brought down considerably, a certain level of sales still had to be achieved, and it had to be considerably more than the discouraging 1957 and 1958 results.

Studebaker needed a new car that would sell, and its only hope was to make whatever car it developed seem all-new. Churchill wisely decided to aim for one of the few industry segments in which there was decent volume and relatively little competition: the compact car market. Product-wise it was a smart move. The Studebaker's body was rather small by full-size car standards (one reason why the cars hadn't sold

Studebaker-Packard President Harold Churchill was the man who conceived the idea of Studebaker getting into the compact market, and he authorized development of the new Lark.

better) but as a compact, its comparatively spacious interior would be a definite competitive advantage. Initially, its only other competitor would be American Motors' Rambler. Since creating a compact would cost relatively little, and the resulting car would compete in a growing market segment against only one other competitor, it was obviously the best move. Considering the alternative, i.e., another rehashing of the same old car, the decision was easy.

Churchill explained what he wanted in the new small car to Eugene Hardig, vice president of engineering, and by September 1957 Hardig had cobbled together a development mule. It was essentially a 1958 sedan with the front and rear ends cut off to give a rough idea of the car's exterior size so stylists would know what they'd have to work with.

THE STATION WAGON

This stunning new station wagon from The Lark Family by Studebaker is roomy enough to meet most any family need, yet small enough to maneuver with an ease you've never known in station wagons before. Engineered and built by the famed craftsmen of Studebaker, it sits comfortably on a sturdy frame uniquely suspended over special "load-leveling" springs on a full 113 inch wheelbase. It's far more economical to run than ordinary station wagons and considerably lower in price. Available with super-economical "6" or ultra-responsive V-8. This one is a pal to Dad, a darling to Mother, a treat to the teenagers, a new favorite for the whole family.

This is the new dimension in station wagons

The station wagon was a popular model in the Lark range. Studebaker offered only a two-door Lark wagon for 1959, an error in light of the popularity of four-door wagons at the time.

WHAT DOES THIS GRILLE SIGNIFY?

➤This grille performs a vital function by admitting an unrestricted flow of air to the radiator. It's an attractive grille by virtue of its entirely functional shape and it signifies what other grilles do not . . . that this is an honest car dealing in fundamentals.
➤The Lark has an unusually high brake lining to weight ratio, and employs an advanced suspension system using variable rate coil springs and hydraulic shocks. Only 14½ feet long, it seats six comfortably and is extremely maneuverable, very easy to park and agile in traffic.
➤Like to work on your own car? The Lark's engine ("6" or V-8) is easily accessible. ➤ Like economy? The Lark V-8 outclassed all V-8's in the Mobilgas Economy Run: 22.28 miles per gallon with automatic transmission. And the "6" does better. ➤Like performance? Try The Lark V-8 with 4-barrel carburetor and dual exhausts. ➤ ➤ Like to drive? Get into a Lark. ➤ See your Studebaker Dealer.

THE *LARK* BY STUDEBAKER

JUNE 1959 **211**

By March 1958, the design staff had completed work on what was termed a "smaller full-size car," which was how AMC marketed its senior Rambler line. While the new car's styling couldn't be called beautiful, it was handsome in a utilitarian way, looked sturdy, and most of all, it appeared all-new, not a rehash or a facelift.

It was, admittedly, a huge gamble. If it failed, Studebaker would be out of the car business forever, and thousands of workers would lose their jobs. If it succeeded, it might spark a renaissance for the old company. A lot was riding on the new Studebaker. This was the last chance for Studebaker to turn things around. The company was down to its last bullet, and this new small car was it. They called it the Lark.

Product-wise, the Lark was neither a copycat nor an imitator. Somehow the company had managed to create a unique product, one with trim exterior dimensions yet boasting a spacious interior and distinctive styling. There were nine models in all. The six-cylinder Lark VI series offered two- and four-door sedans and a two-door wagon in Deluxe trim and a four-door sedan, two-door hardtop, and wagon in costlier Regal trim. The Lark VIII lineup included a four-door sedan, two-door hardtop, and wagon in Regal trim. Despite pocket-size exterior dimensions—at 175 inches in length it was 16 inches shorter than the Rambler Six—the new Lark featured a generous wheelbase of 108.5 inches for sedans and hardtops (half an inch longer than the Rambler)

Here's another view of the sharp 1959 Lark hardtop. Buyers looking for style with economy found it in the six-cylinder Lark. For performance lovers, Lark also offered V8 models that could be equipped with a four-barrel carburetor and dual exhausts.

THE *LARK* BY STUDEBAKER

2 - DOOR SEDAN

This pert, perky and pretty 2-door sedan from The Lark Family by Studebaker is a honey of a jaunter that's some three feet shorter than the low-priced three (and considerably lower in price)...but, surprisingly, provides bountiful seating for six. It rides like a dream, parks on a dime and its six cylinder engine goes miles and miles on a hatful of gas (regular gas, by golly)! Handsomely appointed, practical, easy-to-care-for interiors make this the perfect "beautility" car...ideal for salesmen (and fleets), for shoppers, for teenagers...or for the family's pet second car. *This* is economy with an air of elegance...the 2-door Lark sedan!

This is the new dimension in 2-door sedans

The price leader in the 1959 Lark series was the two-door sedan in Deluxe trim. Although its $1,925 price seemed quite low, it was actually $130 more than the 1958 Scotsman two-door, which sold in the full-size market. The difference was image; Scotsman was a stripped low-buck car while the compact Lark was a smart new idea.

and 113 inches for the station wagon. Prices ranged from $1,925 for the Deluxe two-door Lark VI to $2,590 for the Lark VIII two-door wagon.

There wasn't a four-door wagon in the line, a puzzling oversight in view of the tremendous success AMC was having with them, but overall the lineup was solid and well priced. The standard engine Lark VI was the old 90-horsepower, 169.6-cubic inch flathead six, which was a bit underpowered but smooth running and easy on gas. Lark VIII models got Studebaker's excellent 259-cid V-8, offered in 180- or 195-horsepower versions.

With the Lark's introduction, the company abandoned the full-size car market, walking away from a segment it had occupied for so many years. The inspiration for the Lark had come from the encouraging success of the 1957–'58 Scotsman, and now Lark effectively replaced both the Scotsman and the Champion. Apparently Churchill saw no advantage in also having a big Commander and President in the lineup, which of course would have been possible at

comparatively little cost. Of course, it's unlikely a moderately restyled carryover Commander/President would have sold as well as even 1958's poor showing. However, they might have garnered a decent number of sales from long-time Studebaker loyalists (of which there were thousands) desiring a larger, more traditional Studebaker. Plans were made to discontinue the aging Hawk series, but dealers protested, so the Silver Hawk continued to be offered with a choice of six-cylinder or V-8 power.

The Lark was introduced in the fall of 1958, and within weeks the company knew it had a hit. The new car drew raves from all corners. *Popular Science* called the new Lark "a fresh idea in small cars." The magazine also commented that although the Lark was "sixteen inches shorter than the Rambler, it doesn't have the Rambler's big-car appearance. The Lark looks more like something from Europe."

Churchill, cautiously optimistic, ramped up production volume as dealer orders flowed in. Before long the company also found itself

The Lark four-door sedan for 1959 was offered as a six-cylinder model in Regal or Deluxe trim, or as a V-8 in Regal trim only. Limiting the V-8 models to upper-line Regal trim was an effort to simplify stocking and ordering, but it probably cost the company some sales.

swamped with requests for new dealerships. The Big Three makes had no compact cars, and many of their dealers were clamoring to get in on the compact boom. Studebaker's dealer ranks quickly grew. For the most part, the new dealers were stronger and better financed than the average Studebaker dealer, although as newcomers their loyalty didn't have the same depth. They were coming in on a wave, and only time would tell how long they'd stick around.

Other new products for 1959 included the Econ-O-Miler Taxi, based now on the Lark rather than the Scotsman, as was the case in 1958. Also joining the lineup were a three-passenger Utility Sedan targeting salesmen who needed an inexpensive car with extra carrying space, and the Panel Wagon, a Lark two-door station wagon converted into a panel-delivery. Although unit sales were not large, the fleet models helped add to Studebaker's growing sales volume. The carryover

Although Studebaker considered dropping the Hawk for 1959, dealer protests convinced management to reconsider. The line was trimmed to a single Silver Hawk coupe with a choice of a six or V-8 power.

For 1959 Studebaker's passenger car business was down to essentially two models: the all-new Lark and the carryover Hawk. It was enough; the company turned in the greatest net profit in its history.

truck line offered models ranging from the Scotsman, still America's lowest-priced pickup, to a two-ton heavy hauler. Work also continued on military truck orders.

In June 1959, Studebaker-Packard acquired U.S. distribution rights for the Auto Union–DKW line of vehicles, which would be handled by its wholly owned subsidiary Mercedes-Benz Sales Inc. The line included the DKW 750, a small two-door sedan with a two-stroke three-cylinder engine and a base price of just $1,665. Moving up the ladder in price were the Auto Union cars, offering five models in the 1000 series, all equipped with a three-cylinder engine. They weren't very exciting cars, but the public was extremely interested in import automobiles, and the Auto Union–DKW cars gave Studebaker dealers another line of products to sell. Retail demand for Mercedes-Benz

cars was strong, though sales were held back by tight supplies. Export sales of Studebaker cars and trucks were also on the rise, and contracts were entered into for vehicle assembly in Australia and Israel. Sales in Mexico were up 11 percent over 1958.

What Studebaker accomplished in 1959 was nothing less than a miracle. During the fiscal year, unit sales of cars and trucks rocketed to 182,323, up from 79,301 in 1958. The largest share of this increase occurred in the Studebaker car line. A breakout of 1959 results showed wholesale sales of 160,826 Studebaker cars, 10,909 trucks, and 10,588 Mercedes-Benz/Auto Union vehicles vs. 62,146 cars, 10,735 trucks, and 6,420 Mercedes-Benz units in 1958. Dollar volume more than doubled to $387 million, and income was $28,544,388 compared to 1958's $13.3 million loss. Best of all, because of tax-loss

The Lark station wagon was especially popular with suburbanites. Its combination of utility and economy was perfect for young families.

THE *LARK* BY STUDEBAKER

4-DOOR SEDAN

This is the new dimension in 4-door sedans

Sturdy, spirited, smart and practical in every sense, this 4-door sedan from The Lark Family by Studebaker provides easy access through all four doors and surprises you with its generous headroom and footroom and the spaciousness of its deep, vacation-sized trunk. Costs little to buy, runs miles and miles on a hatful of regular gas, delivers all the power you need, without being wastefully excessive, whether you choose the thrifty "6" or more powerful V-8. Rides in comfort all day, turns and parks on a dime. And it's dependable as it is smart, for it's engineered and built by the famed craftsmen of Studebaker. This is the one...the friendly family car with a wonderful flair all its own.

The Lark was a standout in 1959, and its success rescued Studebaker from almost certain bankruptcy. However, it was able to only temporarily halt the downward slide in car sales, and within eight years the company would exit the automobile business.

(Below) Perhaps not surprising after its first-year success, the Lark returned for 1960 with relatively few changes to the basic car. The grille mesh was changed, and the emblem was now centered at its base.

carry-forward credits it was all tax-free, making it the largest net profit in the company's history. Even more amazing was that this $41.8-million-dollar turnaround was accomplished without having invested in a completely new car.

Corporate assets now included $62 million in cash and marketable securities, up sharply from $35 million the prior year. However, the good news presented management with a question that was difficult to answer: namely, what was the best way to invest this newfound wealth? One significant aspect of the 1958 refinancing and restructuring deal was an agreement by the board of directors that Studebaker would diversify into other fields. The reason given was to cushion and offset as far as possible the cyclical nature of the automotive business. But the finance men also wanted to ensure that if Studebaker were driven out of the auto industry, it would be able to survive in some form. That may strike some as callously ignoring the company's proud history, but the first duty of a board of directors is to protect the stockholders' investment.

To that end, Abraham Sonnabend, a specialist in mergers and acquisitions, was brought in and given a seat on the board, charged with the task of finding companies that Studebaker could acquire. To conserve Studebaker's scarce (and hard-won) cash, these prospective companies needed to be smaller firms with solid balance sheets, good earnings, and a fair amount of cash on hand. It would take time to find companies that fit those criteria and were for sale, but management vowed to spare no effort. In October, Randolph Guthrie, a senior partner in the law firm of Mudge, Stern, Baldwin and Todd, U.S. legal counsel for Daimler-Benz, was also elected to the board of directors.

The first acquisition was Cincinnati Testing Laboratories Inc. (CTL), a specialty plastics research and manufacturing operation. CTL produced the nose cones for the Titan, Jupiter, and Pershing missiles.

One welcome addition to the Lark lineup was this four-door station wagon, available as a six- or eight-cylinder model in Deluxe or Regal trim. Four-door compact wagons were very popular at the time, and the new Lark wagon sold well.

Another new addition to the expanded Lark series was this lovely Lark convertible. As a top-line model, the convertible came only in Regal trim but could be ordered with either a six or V-8 engine. The convertible models are highly prized today.

Gering Plastics Inc., a volume producer of plastic compounds and polyethylene films, was also acquired. It was important that Studebaker move quickly to acquire other companies.

At the end of 1959, the company had well over $100 million in tax-loss carry-forward credits that could be applied to offset taxable profits in the coming years. Since Curtiss-Wright hadn't gone through with the merger, those tax credits were available for Studebaker-Packard's use. They could be used to offset future profits, including those of acquired companies, in effect allowing Studebaker to acquire profitable firms and use a portion of those companies' own profits to help fund the acquisitions program. However, the tax losses had a five-year life span, so the company needed to utilize them before they expired. The approximate amounts available and their expiration dates were as follows:

Amount	Date of Expiration
$15 million	December 31, 1960
$34 million	December 31, 1961
$27 million	December 31, 1962
$33 million	December 31, 1963

It was mainly because of these credits that Harold Churchill, favorite son and hero of South Bend and savior of Studebaker-Packard in 1959, found himself under intense pressure in 1960. His directors were pushing

The Hawk returned to the line for 1960, again with little change. Rightly or wrongly, the company was focusing its efforts on the Lark, so the Hawk was left to fend for itself. The "Silver" part of the name was dropped, and this year the Hawk was available only with a V-8.

him to acquire more companies and diversify Studebaker-Packard as rapidly as possible. There were arguments over what sort of new cars to develop and even whether or not to bother investing in new cars.

Competition was a lot tougher in 1960 because the Big Three had entered the compact market in force. Chevrolet introduced its new Corvair, Ford debuted its Falcon, Mercury the stylish Comet, and Plymouth its Valiant. Sales of AMC's Rambler were red-hot, and plainly the competitive field was drastically altered from the prior year.

In addition, many of Churchill's dealers were suddenly deserting him. Old-line dealers, the ones who'd weathered so much and managed to hang on, were still there for the most part. But scores of newer dealers, primarily the Big Three retailers who'd signed up to sell the Lark in 1959, dropped their franchises when the corporate divisions that produced their primary brands suddenly jumped into the compact field. Mercury dealers cancelled their Studebaker franchises to concentrate on the Comet, Chevy dealers dropped the Lark in favor of the Corvair, and

so forth. The loss in quantity and quality of outlets hurt the company's ability to sell more cars. There were charges that certain Big Three divisions were actively luring old-line Studebaker dealers to drop their Studebaker-Packard franchises and take on theirs.

Against the all-new competitors Studebaker had only its Lark, a second-year car with a few new features, a couple new body styles, and some styling revisions. Up front the Lark received a new grille and emblem. Two new body styles debuted, an attractive convertible and, overdue but welcome nonetheless, a four-door station wagon.

The model range was expanded, a good idea since during the previous year the range had been rather narrow. To illustrate, in 1959 V-8 models were offered only in the more expensive Regal trim, which price-wise was about $130 more than the Deluxe series. While that may not sound like much, it represented a nearly 6 percent premium, making the V-8s cost more than many families were willing to pay. But for 1960, the V-8 series offered two- and four-door sedans and two- and

A smart move by Churchill in 1960 was to introduce an all-new light pickup based on Lark sheet metal. This gave dealers a modern-looking truck with terrific style. *Photo courtesy Mike Mueller*

four-door wagons, in both Deluxe and Regal trim. The Hawk carried over with minimal changes: the *"Silver"* part of the name was dropped and the 289 V-8 was now the standard engine, with 210 horsepower standard, 225 horsepower optional.

On the truck front, the company introduced the new Champ pickup. Using Lark sheet metal, Champ offered a stylish cab with a vastly more modern appearance. Champ was an attractive entry in the light-duty pickup field and welcomed by dealers and the public.

Churchill was optimistic that Studebaker's auto business had turned the corner and would once more be a force in the auto industry,

and 1959 certainly encouraged his belief. But the Lark's success in 1959 created another crossroads for the company. The board had to decide to either pour the profits back into the car business or use them to diversify, ensuring the survival of the corporation. Churchill argued to do both, angering several on the board who felt the best use of the money was to acquire more businesses. Both arguments had valid points to consider, but in the end the sales results for 1960 may have decided the case.

Initially, it appeared that Lark sales would hold up. The company continued to produce cars at a high rate, filling dealer orders that had been placed months earlier. But gradually the inflow of new orders

(Right) Another top-line model for 1960 was the sweet-looking Lark hardtop. Available only in Regal trim, the hardtop offered both six and V-8 engines. Despite the additions to the model lineup, Lark sales fell in 1960, a victim of increased competition in the compact segment.

Entering its sixth year in production was the 1961 Studebaker Hawk shown here. As good a road machine as it was, there had been little change over the years, and the Hawk was no longer the attention-getter it once had been. However, Hawk boasted a solid core of enthusiast owners, and sales, though low, were fairly steady.

Announcing the new Gran Turismo Studebaker Hawk in limited number only for 1961—*with 4-speed gearbox**

James Mason has Hawk Number 12 Mr. Mason has added a Hawk to his collection of exemplary motor cars which includes a Rolls Royce and an Alvis from Great Britain.

His reason is that The Hawk prescribes motoring pleasure as no other American car can. Think of its powerful V-8 engine, its smooth 4-speed gearbox*, its contoured bucket seats and best of all, its soul-satisfying performance and controllability.

This is motoring in the modern manner: High average cruising speeds in the Continental Gran Turismo fashion, with luxurious accommodations for five. Every Hawk has its owner's name and the car number engraved on a special instrument panel plaque.

Visit your Studebaker Dealer and place your order now.   *Optional

The Hawk is also manufactured and sold in Canada.

From the beginning Studebaker Hawk earned a reputation as a driver's car. For 1961 its performance was enhanced by the addition of a four-speed gearbox to the option list. Here, actor James Mason—the villain in the great Hitchcock film *North by Northwest*—poses with his own personal Hawk.

began to lessen, and production had to be cut back in order to reduce bloated inventories. Although model year production was off only by a few thousand, calendar year production and sales to dealers fell significantly. For the fiscal year, Studebaker produced 109,781 cars compared to 160,826 the prior year. The reason for the drop was easy to see. In 1959 there had been only Rambler and Studebaker in the compact field, but before the end of the 1960 calendar year, 11 domestic makes were competing there. In a suddenly crowded market segment Studebaker once more found itself being squeezed.

Mercedes-Benz sales provided a bright spot. Although unit sales of 12,687 were up just 5 percent, the import market had suffered a sharp downturn. By the final quarter, Mercedes-Benz was in third place in import sales, topped only by two low-priced makes. On the other hand, sales of DK–Auto Union cars proved disappointing.

The Lark VIII convertible for 1961. Frontal appearance was made more handsome by a new fine-mesh grille, along with quad headlamps on Regal and Cruiser models.

For 1960, the corporation sold a total of 133,984 cars and trucks, down from 182,323 in 1959. The Automotive Division lost money for the year, but because of its acquired divisions the company managed to report a net profit of $708,850. Tax-loss carry-forwards meant the profit was tax-free; good news, yes, but millions in tax credits expired unused.

During the year, Studebaker-Packard acquired three very good companies, each a leader in its respective field. Clarke Floor Machines of Muskegon, Michigan, produced a diversified line of floor finishing and maintenance equipment. D. W. Onan and Sons of Minneapolis manufactured a broad range of electric generating plants. Gravely Tractors of Dunbar, West Virginia, manufactured small utility tractors for lawn, garden, and farm applications.

Since Studebaker-Packard continued to suffer heavy losses in its automotive operations, some board members argued for exiting the auto business. Churchill strongly opposed this and fought for spending more to introduce new automobiles. By the end of 1960, the board decided a change was in order. A search was begun for a new president who would focus more on acquisitions. Using accumulated tax losses to offset the subsidiary's profits would boost the bottom line and provide more cash for further acquisitions. The problem was it would likely sound the death knell for Studebaker-Packard's car business.

By the end of the year, company management underwent a drastic overhaul. On September 2, 1960, Hugh Ferry, the former Packard executive who served as Studebaker-Packard chairman, was replaced by Clarence Francis. At 72, Francis was old to be running a major company beset by so many problems, and he vowed to search for a younger man to handle the day-to-day running of the firm. In addition to focusing on the crucial acquisitions program, Francis wanted a dynamic, powerful leader able to take charge of the company and guide it to safer ground. By the end of the year, he'd found the man he wanted. In February 1961, Harold Churchill stepped down as president, to be replaced by Sherwood H. Egbert, who came from McCulloch Corporation, manufacturer of chain saws and outboard engines. Egbert became president and chief executive officer of Studebaker-Packard Corporation effective February 1, 1961.

There had been a power struggle prior to Egbert's hiring. A. M. Sonnabend wanted to be president and promised to lead an aggressive acquisitions program while putting Churchill in command of the auto division. Vice President D. Ray Hall, who'd joined Studebaker as part of the Gravely acquisition, also wanted the top job. At first the board seemed ready to choose Sonnabend, then backed off and agreed to meet again in a few days to reconsider the matter. When they met December 28, the majority of votes were for Egbert. An angry Sonnabend thereupon declared, "The decision is ridiculous. The board should disband, get out. It is worthless!" When the board met with Egbert the following month, Sonnabend tendered his resignation.

Styling changes on the 1961 Lark series included a new flatter, roof panel and a lower cowl, hood, and rear deck. The quad lamps, fine-mesh grille, and bright exterior moldings on this hardtop add much to its appeal.

Egbert was a hard charger, an ex-marine who liked businesses run his way. Consensus management was not his style. He shook things up in South Bend, patrolling offices late at night and in the early morning, asking questions, ordering changes. Before long, Studebaker's tired old plant was given a new coat of paint courtesy of assembly line workers using leftover automotive paint. In a whirlwind series of meetings, Egbert spoke personally with some 700 Studebaker dealers, soliciting suggestions for improving sales. He instituted further cost-cutting measures to reduce overhead and laid out a four-part plan to restore the company to profitability. These included:

(1) Continuing and expanding the acquisitions program vital to the company's future. Millions in tax carry-forwards had already expired unused.

(2) Strengthening the automotive division's competitive position. The fastest road to recovery was to eliminate the losses the automotive division was incurring. While a reduction in overhead helped, a strong sales improvement could spark a major recovery.

On September 2, 1960, Hugh Ferry was replaced as chairman of Studebaker-Packard by 72-year-old Clarence Francis (right). Then, in early 1961, Sherwood H. Egbert (left), formerly with McCulloch Corporation, replaced Harold Churchill as company president. Egbert was named president and chief executive officer of the Studebaker-Packard Corporation effective February 1, 1961.

(3) Seeking a larger share of military business. Studebaker was producing trucks; Egbert told his staff to seek out any kind of manufacturing contracts, from missiles to mess kits.

(4) Setting up an International Division focusing on sales of the company's broad range of products in overseas market. These would include the products of the acquired divisions.

When Egbert arrived at Studebaker-Packard midway through the 1961 model year, car sales were down significantly from the lamentable 1960 results. One reason was that the U.S. auto industry was experiencing a downturn. Every company was affected, but Studebaker-Packard's loss was more noticeable because of the company's fragile condition. Rumors that Studebaker was about to go out of business were flying everywhere, and that hurt sales even more.

The 1961 Larks had a lot going for them. A new 112-horsepower Skybolt six-cylinder overhead-valve engine debuted. Based on the prior flathead six, it offered greatly increased power along with claims of improved fuel economy.

Styling changes included a new, flatter roof panel, along with a lowered cowl, hood, and rear deck. Frontal appearance was made more handsome by a new fine-mesh grille, along with quad headlamps on Regal and Cruiser models. Side moldings were revised, and a new Cruiser long-wheelbase, V-8–powered, four-door sedan debuted in the Lark VIII series. This interesting model, 4 inches longer than a standard Lark, rode the wagon's longer 113-inch wheelbase.

The Cruiser provided generous interior space with trim exterior dimensions and decent economy. A 259-cid V-8 and fancy interior trim were standard equipment. The fading Hawk line returned with little exterior change but now offered a Warner Gear four-speed transmission (the same one Corvette used). Hawk also offered new contoured bucket seats.

Meanwhile, of course, the acquisitions program continued. On March 1, 1961, Chemical Compounds Inc. of St. Joseph, Missouri, maker of STP Oil Treatment, was acquired. By now, total annual sales for all of Studebaker-Packard's acquired divisions was running about $100 million annually. The search for more companies continued, with Egbert now leading the way.

Notice the dual headlamps of this Lark VI two-door sedan. The two-door sedan came only in basic Deluxe trim, which came standard with two headlamps, while fancier versions came with quad lamps. This seemingly minor touch made a great deal of difference in the Lark's appearance.

For 1961 a new Cruiser sedan debuted in the Lark VIII series. Four inches longer than the standard Lark, the Cruiser was based on the wagon's longer 113-inch wheelbase. The new model offered generous interior space with trim exterior dimensions. Cruisers came with a standard 259-cid V-8 and upscale interior trim.

During the year Egbert concentrated on improving the dealer network, weeding out weak dealers and replacing them with stronger ones with higher potential volume. At the end of 1961, the company had 2,102 dealers, signing 180 new ones in the last four months of the year. Egbert also authorized the establishment of factory retail outlets to improve representation in large metropolitan markets where it had few dealerships.

Studebaker introduced another innovation in 1961, being the first U.S. builder to offer a line of medium-duty trucks with factory-installed diesel engines. Offering greatly reduced operating costs, the diesel trucks sold well. And of course, one has only to note that today nearly all such trucks are diesel-powered.

In May, Egbert announced that the entire 1961 model run was sold out. His statement sounded more impressive than it actually was. After all, car companies generally book their final orders for the model year around June. Usually, a dealer's final year order covers the last two months of production—roughly between June and August. After that, production commences on the next model year cars in order to have a good supply in

time for a September/October introduction. Leaving off the gingerbread, what Egbert's statement really meant was that his dealers had ordered the final cars from their reduced allotment about a month earlier than normal. In light of the harsh fact that overall sales fell for the year, Egbert's pronouncement meant relatively little. But it sure sounded good.

During the year, the company bought back the Chippewa Avenue plant it had sold to Curtiss-Wright, whose Utica-Bend Division was already history. It was to be the new home of Studebaker-Packard's Defense Products Division.

Mercedes-Benz retail sales reached an all-time high in 1961: 12,637 units. Auto Union–DKW sales continued to disappoint, so a lower-priced model was being readied for fall introduction.

Studebaker-Packard's operating results for 1961 were rather poor, but the company reported a net profit overall, so it looked like an improvement. Total unit sales of cars and trucks fell to 102,932 versus 133,984 the prior year, a 23 percent drop. Dollar volume fell to $298 million, down $25 million. The automotive division continued to lose money, causing the entire company to suffer an operating loss of $3.1 million for the year.

The good-looking Lark station wagon was offered in two- and four-door models for 1961. Though costlier, the four-door wagons outsold the two-door versions by a wide margin. With plenty of room plus outstanding economy, they were a favorite among young families.

However, the Gering Plastics Division was sold during the year, netting an excellent profit of $5.66 million on the deal. That nonrecurring profit more than offset the operating loss, so the company was able to report a net profit of $2.535 million for 1961. Even better was the news that during the final quarter of 1961, the company was once again profitable on an operating basis. In all, including the nonrecurring income from the Gering sale, Studebaker-Packard showed a fourth-quarter profit of $12.8 million. Business was picking up. Apparently, the public was encouraged by the new management team and the growing improvement in the company's overall sales.

Studebaker-Packard appeared finally to be in recovery. Car sales were up, each of the acquired divisions was operating profitably, and the person leading the company was a hard-driving individual determined

to win. The big gamble on the Lark had brought in cash and bought the company some time. The gamble on the acquisitions program had worked, perhaps not as well as the golden dreams of A. M. Sonnabend, but enough to provide a firm foundation for growth.

And the gamble on Sherwood Egbert had worked out. Egbert brought in two designers charged with revitalizing Studebaker's automobiles, to drive up sales and restore the auto division's health. Because of the company's precarious position, the designers wouldn't have the usual two to three years to develop new cars. Egbert wanted new products on the floor, and he wanted them now. Design work would need somehow to be compressed from years or months into weeks. And with contracts up for renewal, the union would also need to do its part. It was vital.

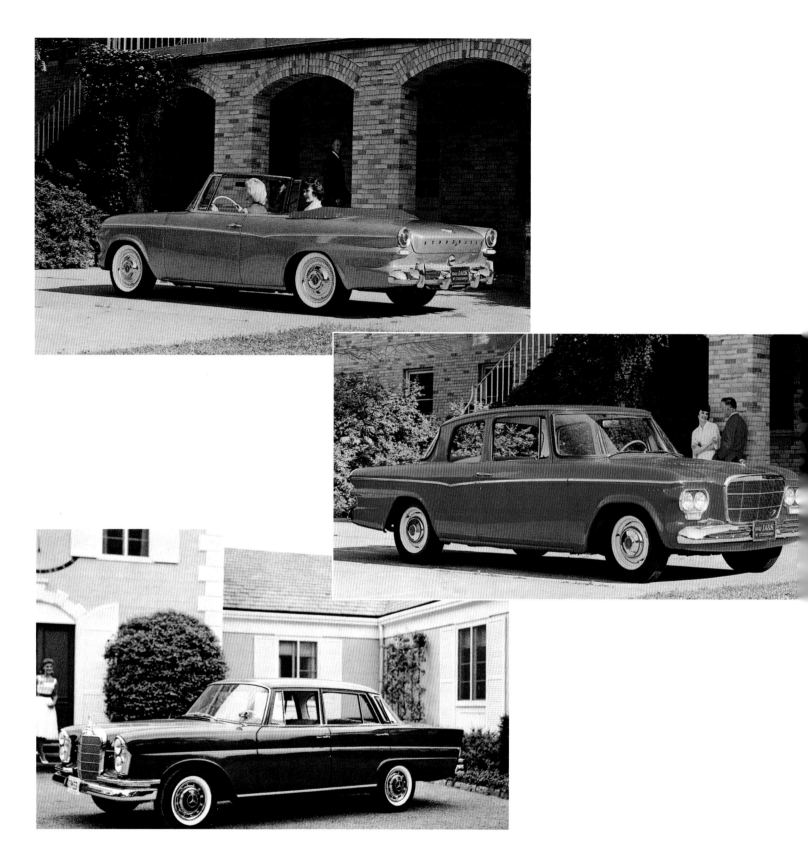

Here are three of the exciting automotive products offered by Studebaker-Packard for 1962. The Lark convertible shows its sassy new lines to good advantage, while the Lark two-door sedan looks richer than before with its greater length plus a new grille and frontal styling. The Mercedes-Benz 220 sedan was one of the most popular import cars that year.

CHAPTER SEVEN

1962-1966
It All Falls Apart

Two of Studebaker's great surprises for 1962 arrived in the fall of 1961, when the 1962 new car line-up was announced to the public. Automotive journalists hadn't anticipated much from Studebaker-Packard; since the company had no money they expected only minor variations on the Lark. But the 1962 Lark was quite different from previous models; it looked almost completely new.

The new car was, however, merely a clever facelift of the 1961. The stylist, industrial designer Brooks Stevens, had used his budget creatively. Buyers disliked the old Lark's short and stubby appearance, so a new front-end panel was grafted on, extending the grille area forward. The grille itself was larger and richer looking, with fine mesh divided by bright trim bars, quite similar to the concurrent Mercedes-Benz. Side moldings were placed lower on the bodyside, giving the whole car a lower look. Quad headlamps became standard on all models.

A bigger change was in the overall length. New rear styling included longer fenders and deck, giving the Lark a more graceful look. Wheelbase was increased to 109 inches on all two-door models except wagons, while all four-door sedans now rode the same 113-inch platform as Cruisers and wagons. Overall length on two-doors was 9 inches longer than before, while four-door sedans were 13 inches greater. A new Skytop sunroof became available. It was a very successful facelift on an extremely limited budget.

There was a sharp new series this year called the Daytona. Its appearance was testimony that although Egbert may not have had an automotive background, at heart he was an enthusiast. Daytona was Studebaker's entry in the new sporty compact segment. Equipment included standard bucket seats, center console, and full carpeting, plus available four-speed transmission and bigger 289-cid V-8 with 210 horsepower or 225 horsepower. Styling touches included an interesting side molding with gold Daytona script.

But a bigger surprise that season was when Studebaker unveiled a restyled Hawk. Brooks Stevens made it look completely new and extremely attractive, though in fact it was only a relatively inexpensive facelift. Using the old hardtop body, Stevens cut off the Hawk's fins and replaced the rounded roof with a longer and flatter roofline, giving it a completely new silhouette similar to the Ford Thunderbird. The crisp new roof also provided greatly increased interior roominess. Stevens also redesigned many small items like taillamps and moldings, but the roof and rear fenders constituted the greatest change.

Sherwood H. Egbert, president of Studebaker-Packard Corporation, was given the job of diversifying the company out of the automobile business. Once at the helm, however, Egbert made strenuous efforts to save the car division.

(Below) Stevens was the genius behind the restyled 1962 Larks. His design budget was miniscule, but despite that Stevens was able to greatly improve the Lark's styling. This new Lark Daytona sports model was introduced that same year with bucket seats and stylish trim.

'62 Lark 2-door Sedan

'62 Lark Cruiser

'62 Lark 4-door Sedan

'62 Lark Daytona Convertible
also standard model

'62 Lark Daytona Hardtop
also standard model

'62 Lark Station Wagon

Gran Turismo Hawk '62

'62 Studebaker taxicab

'62 Studebaker Marshal
police special

'62 Champ ¼ ton pickup

'62 Transtar 2-ton platform

'62 Studebaker Diesel
Medium-weight class

This spread illustrates the many facets of Studebaker-Packard's automotive division. In addition to these U.S.–built models, the company also sold Mercedes-Benz cars, plus the Auto Union–DKW line.

Under Egbert's command, Studebaker-Packard's automotive division began to renovate its automobiles and trucks. Despite having only a modest budget to work with, the Gran Turismo Hawk designed by Brooks Stevens was a styling tour de force. Introduced as a 1962 model, it received wide acclaim from journalists who tested it.

The new Hawk was a fashionable grand tourer, the sort of car usually available only from Europe, and it arrived with a considerable price increase: $3095 base price versus $2650 for the '61 model. Management decided the revised car deserved a new name, so it was dubbed the Gran Turismo (Grand Touring) Hawk. Its continental styling won raves, and the standard V-8 and performance options meant the GT Hawk wasn't just a pretty face; it offered outstanding speed and handling as well.

Midway through the year came an even greater surprise. Egbert announced an all-new sporty car called the Avanti would arrive later that year. It was meant to be a halo car, a high-performance sports coupe whose stunningly beautiful lines would cast a halo of reflected glamour and excitement over the other Studebaker cars.

The public had never seen anything like the Avanti before. It was sleek and low, yet it offered room for four passengers and their luggage. At first glance, there appeared to be no grille opening, just a smooth nose jutting forward. Avanti had a fiberglass body like the Corvette, a standard V-8 engine, optional supercharger and four-speed transmission, and standard bucket seats equal to the best Europe had to offer. It bristled with innovation, offering an aircraft-inspired overhead console, red instrument panel lighting, concealed safety roll bar, and standard front disc brakes.

Avanti remains one of the most beautiful automobiles ever to grace the road. The moving force behind it was, again, Egbert. He wanted something bold to attract attention to Studebaker products,

One of the most beautiful road cars of the 1960s was the Gran Turismo Hawk. Available only as a V-8 hardtop coupe, the GT Hawk won wide acclaim. Undoubtedly, if the public wasn't so worried about Studebaker going out of business, many more Hawks would have been purchased.

Frontal view of the beautiful Gran Turismo Hawk for 1962 shows the understated elegance of Stevens' design. These unique cars were powerful, competent road machines, offering European standards of road handling with American power and quality. Owner: Jay Cowperthwaite.

acting like a magnet to draw buyers to his dealers. On an airplane trip, he jotted down some ideas of what sort of car it should be. He contacted Raymond Loewy, giving him the task of turning those thoughts into an actual car. Loewy sent a small team of designers to a rented home in Palm Springs, California, and over a period of six weeks they created the masterful design. Egbert had wanted a two-seater, but Engineering Vice President Hardig convinced him to make it a four-seater.

The Avanti was something utterly unique for an American company, a true four-place grand touring coupe with stunning looks and breathtaking appearance. Dramatically styled and blisteringly fast, Studebaker's hot new car was a triumph of advanced thinking and design. Perhaps the only cars close to it in concept were exotics like the Aston Martin, Bristol, or Jaguar. But they were European and Avanti was American, the only American car in the high-performance grand touring niche. Talk about style: although James Bond drove an Aston Martin, his creator, Ian Fleming, drove an Avanti.

Although all Lark four-door sedans rode the 113-inch wheelbase this year, the Cruiser models were easy to spot by the six-window greenhouse. Cruiser continued to offer a fancier interior.

The exciting 1963 Studebaker Avanti was one of the most beautiful sports coupes ever produced. *Photo courtesy Mike Mueller*

Once Sherwood Egbert decided Studebaker needed a sports car to draw attention to its product offerings, he hired Raymond Loewy to design the new car—which would be named Avanti—on a crash basis. Here Loewy works a clay model of one idea.

Three of the four-member Avanti design team. Left to right are Tom Kellogg, Raymond Loewy, and John Epstein, shown outside the California desert home where the Avanti was created.

The unexpectedly stylish cars for 1962 surprised many who were predicting Studebaker's imminent collapse. These cars came about because Egbert listened to dealers and pushed through the changes in record time. And because he brought in the two outside designers, Stevens and Loewy, to ramrod the changes.

One alteration people viewed with mixed feelings was a change in the company name. The directors felt that including Packard as part of the corporation's name was harming business, since it was a reminder that the company's other car brand was an orphan. Accordingly, on April 26, 1962, the company was renamed, once more becoming the Studebaker Corporation. The board noted that "While at one time Packard had been a great name, it is presently associated by the public with a defunct company and this is hurting the Corporation."

Studebaker acquired four additional companies during the year at an investment of $47 million. Franklin Manufacturing Company of

Initially, Egbert wanted Avanti to be a two-place sports car like the Corvette, and this lovely design is one that was considered. Engineering Vice President Eugene Hardig convinced him to make it a four-place grand tourer.

According to John Epstein, Raymond Loewy insisted the new car have blade-type front fenders. The designers were also instructed to investigate having a foil-type grille similar to the Lincoln Continental. This drawing shows both ideas, along with quad headlamps.

Even while the design was still in the two-passenger phase (before it was decided that Avanti would be a four-passenger sport coupe), the basic theme for the rear styling was beginning to take form.

The four-man team that created the Avanti is pictured outside the Palm Springs rented home where the Avanti was born. From left are Tom Kellogg, Raymond Loewy, Bob Andrews, and John Epstein.

Minneapolis produced home appliances for private label sale, meaning they were marketed under store brands or private brands rather than under the Franklin name. Operating seven plants with more than a million and a half square feet devoted to manufacturing, Franklin was the largest acquisition to date and cost Studebaker quite a bit, reportedly $41 million.

Other acquisitions included Domowatt S.P.A., an Italian appliance maker, acquired in the belief it had tremendous potential for expanded sales in Europe and could serve as a base for Franklin's overseas sales. Trans International Airlines was a small airline engaged as a contract carrier for the military, flying routes from California to Pacific bases. TIA's fleet consisted of four aircraft, only one of which was a jet. The other acquisition was Schaefer, a top-ranked manufacturer of commercial ice cream, frozen food, and dairy equipment. Like Franklin, Schaefer was based in Minneapolis.

Notice the attractive side molding on this 1962 Studebaker Daytona hardtop. Sporty compacts were in strong demand in 1962, and Studebaker was able to field a good-looking and very competitive car.

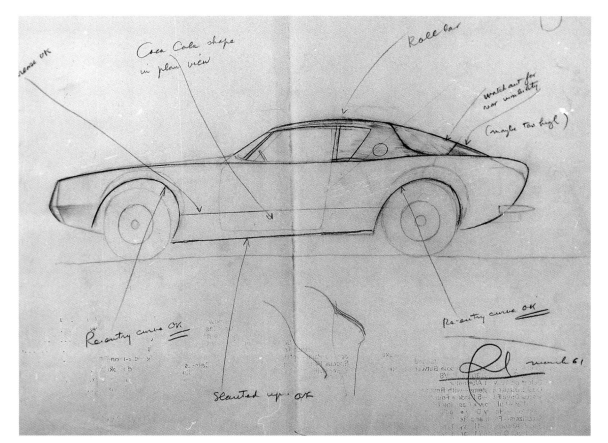

In this drawing we see the four-place Avanti's shape coming together. There was still much detail work to do, but the basic car was there.

After the designers made a small clay it was sent to South Bend, where company design staff created a full-size clay. Note the Lark in the background.

(Above) Egbert was extremely pleased with the Avanti. Here he stands proudly next to the new car, resting a hand on the roof, with a beaming Raymond Loewy next to him.

(Left) It wasn't often that *Motor Trend* magazine put a Studebaker on the front cover, but the beautiful new Avanti rated a turn. It appeared in the July 1962 issue, a proud symbol of the company's determination to remain in the automobile business.

The Mercedes-Benz line continued as one of the most popular import brands in America. Many of today's Mercedes-Benz dealers got their start with Studebaker.

At the internationally renowned Schloss Mittersill Sport and Gun Club overlooking Austria's beautiful Salzach Valley

This is the Way to See Europe...and America Too

You can travel First Class on the road at an advantageous price, if you take delivery of a Mercedes-Benz in Europe. Your car will be delivered to you at the factory in Stuttgart or in virtually any principal city in Europe. You will find your Mercedes-Benz a passport to a perfect trip. Wherever you go or stay in Europe, you are received as befits the owner of a Mercedes-Benz, which is the car of people of state and stateliness. Go in the autumn or the winter when far fewer tourists encroach on your privacy. Sightsee or ski but add a Mercedes-Benz to your pleasure. You will find that motoring behind the silver, three-pointed star of Mercedes-Benz is the most distinguished and comfortable way to get to the other end of a road...in Europe or the U.S.A.

Mercedes-Benz Sales, Inc., South Bend, Indiana
(A Subsidiary of Studebaker-Packard Corporation)

One additional acquisition that year, beyond the four already detailed, was Paxton Products of Santa Monica, California, maker of the Paxton supercharger. Egbert realized Studebaker was in danger of falling behind in the industry's horsepower race. Lacking the funds for new engines, the supercharger would keep Studebaker competitive performancewise, at least for a few years. Paxton's president was Andy Granatelli: racer, engineer, and one of America's top performance experts.

During 1962, Studebaker produced 99,476 cars and trucks in the United States and Canada, an 8 percent gain over the 92,434 built the prior year. Retail sales in the United States for the period were 77,877 cars and 5,899 trucks, both up. Mercedes-Benz Sales Inc. had a good year, too, selling 13,300 Mercedes-Benz cars, a new record. DKW sales remained low, however. The new DKW Junior, introduced for 1962 to replace the unsuccessful DKW 750, failed to achieve volume sales despite a more powerful engine, improved trim, and lower $1,595 base price. In November, Studebaker expanded its import base, acquiring distribution rights for Mercedes-Benz and DKW in Canada.

Avantis away! Two truckloads of new Avantis leave South Bend on their way to dealers across the country.

The Avanti's main purpose was to inject some excitement into the line and draw customers to Studebaker showrooms, where they might purchase a new Lark or GT Hawk. But the Avanti was also supposed to sell in fair numbers; management mentioned 12,000 per year, which certainly wasn't unreasonable.

For the year, the company reported a net profit of $2.56 million, a bit more than 1961. However, one major difference was that 1962's results included an operating profit of $489,000, while an operating loss of $3.1 million had been recorded for 1961. Both years benefited from nonrecurring income: $2 million for 1962 and $5.66 million for 1961. The good news was that the diversification program was obviously working. The company was able to report a profit even in the face of continued losses in the auto division. The bad news was that the auto division had lost money despite all the effort to develop new products.

Incredibly, Studebaker's own workers were the main cause of the auto division's losses. In January 1962, they went out on strike, shutting down South Bend operations for 38 days. One has to wonder if the workers had any grasp on reality. The reality for the auto division was that since 1953, it had earned a significant profit only once. Reality was that the plant was old and rundown, lacking the latest machinery and processes. With high overhead and low sales, the auto division had only a slim chance of earning a profit, and the strike killed that. To strike the company when it was so close to igniting a recovery was a serious mistake.

Studebaker had expended sufficient money and effort to turn the auto business around in 1962. But for 38 precious days no cars were built, as inventory stood uselessly waiting on the line, and Studebaker bled. Worse, after reading about the strike, thousands of potential buyers stayed away from Studebaker dealers, believing there wouldn't be

Studebaker-Packard President Sherwood Egbert is shown with the only all-new car he was able to develop in his tenure. Despite its tremendous appeal, the Avanti didn't sell in sufficient numbers to make it a viable product.

The Lark for 1963 received more revisions in an attempt to keep it fresh. The grille was new, as was the grille emblem. Note the amber turn lenses, also new for 1963.

Looking at the 1963 Lark head-on one sees the flatter windshield glass that replaced the wraparound window and eliminated the troublesome dogleg. The flatter, more modern roof panel is also visible.

cars available. It showed clearly in the monthly sales totals for 1962. In the first nine months of the year, the only two down months were the strike months of January and February. All other months through September showed dramatic increases. The strike cost millions in lost revenue and hurt morale throughout the company and the dealer network. One can only imagine how much better the corporation might have done during 1962 if its auto division hadn't lost more than a month of income.

The dispute was over the usual items that are subject to negotiation: vacation pay, shift premiums, and the amount of clean-up time employees were allowed. For years, workers had enjoyed more daily clean-up time than the average, and Studebaker hoped to cut that by 15 minutes. In the end, a compromise was reached, and the company won back only five minutes. Sadly, the loss of confidence caused by the strike may have been the straw that finally broke the auto division.

After all the changes created for the 1962 models, the 1963 models had to be mainly carryover. However, Brooks Stevens was able to update them on a shoestring budget, giving them a more contemporary look. The Lark's greenhouse—the upper structure— was completely redesigned. On doors, the upper window frames

The Lark model range for 1963 included the base Standard series, the Regal shown here, and the new top-line Custom series. Above the Custom was the sporty Daytona. The most expensive four-door sedan was the Cruiser, offered in a single V-8 four-door model.

Studebaker's long history as an automobile producer was highlighted in this press photograph showing the new 1963 Studebaker Lark alongside a circa-1903 Studebaker Electric.

One of Studebaker's more interesting innovations was the sliding-roof station wagon, introduced on the 1963 Wagonaire. Designed by Brooks Stevens, the sliding roof attracted a lot of attention, and production increased slightly over the 1962 model, one of few bright spots in the 1963 model run.

were made thinner, imparting a lighter, airier look. The windshield frame was squared up and a flatter window installed, doing away with the severe wraparound windshield and attendant dogleg that occasionally barked the knees of the inattentive. Roof C pillars were wider, and a flatter window replaced the wraparound rear glass. The grille had finer mesh, and there were other minor changes. Three trim levels were offered at first: Regal, Custom, and Daytona. The Standard series was added midyear. It offered several stripped-down models with prices starting at $1,935.

Two-door station wagons were dropped, while the four-door wagons debuted an interesting innovation. The new Wagonaire featured a sliding rear roof section that allowed tall items like refrigerators to be carried upright. All a driver needed to do was slide the roof forward to create a sort of mini-pickup. It was handy, but water leaks delayed production while new seals were engineered. A fixed-roof option eventually became available for $100 less. Updated interiors boasted new instrument panels with a slide-out vanity that included built-in drink holders and a pop-up makeup mirror.

Studebaker Canada advertising and public relations manager Paul Durish presents the keys to a new 1963 Lark convertible to lovely Jane Kmita, Miss Dominion of Canada, for use in all her Miss Dominion of Canada appearances.

Avanti was supposed to be the big 1963 model news, but problems had delayed production considerably. The original plan was to produce several thousand Avantis by August 1962, but even by September the plant was assembling only about ten cars a day. Many impatient buyers cancelled their orders, and dealers eventually lost faith in the car. However, even after the problems were finally worked out and cars were readily available, management found it had greatly overestimated the public's interest. Despite its stunning beauty, Avanti (of which Studebaker hoped to sell 12,000 or more per year) was a sales flop.

Egbert thought a performance image might spur Lark and Hawk sales, so Avanti engines became available in both. The R-1 engine included a three-quarter race cam, heavy-duty valves, four-barrel carb, and 10.25:1 compression. The R-2 engine came with a Paxton supercharger. Dubbed the Super Lark and Super Hawk, they offered incredible performance.

During the year, Paxton President Andy Granatelli brought a team of drivers and a fleet of Studebaker cars to the Bonneville Salt Flats hoping to break a few performance records. They set 72 new United States Auto Club (USAC) records including 118.33 miles per hour for 500 kilometers, a flying 50-kilometer run of 155 miles per hour, and an E-Supercharged class run at 147.36 miles per hour. A supercharged Daytona convertible shot through the traps at 153.48 miles per hour. Topping the week was when an Avanti driven by Granatelli himself scorched the salt with an incredible recording-setting run, a 170.8-miles-per-hour average for the American Class C Closed Car Supercharged and American Unlimited Class Closed Car categories. It was a mind-blowing performance.

But soon after introduction of the 1963 line, sales began to slip, and as the months went by the slide accelerated. Sales during September 1962 were slightly above the prior year, but October

The name is Fleming—Ian Fleming. Here the James Bond creator/author poses with his Avanti coupe.

The 1963 Lark Regal two-door was a value model, offering much nicer trim than the Standard Larks and a much more attractive price than the high-style Custom Larks. The new roofline and flatter windshield are easy to spot here.

The interior trim on the Daytona series was unusually attractive. Bucket seats, console, and plush upholstery were features.

1962 saw fewer Studebakers retailed than October 1961. November and December were also down. The decline continued into 1963, each month recording fewer sales than the previous year, except on two occasions. February showed a gain because a year earlier sales had been held down by the strike. October 1963 also showed a gain right after the 1964 models went on sale. With those two exceptions, 1963 was a disaster. U.S. retail car sales fell to 64,570, a 17 percent decline and far below the company's still-too-high break-even point. Truck sales dropped to 5,422 units. What had happened?

There were many causes for the drop-off in sales. The compact market continued to be a hotly contested battleground. Chevy fielded Corvair and Chevy II compacts and late in 1963 introduced a new Chevelle on a 115-inch wheelbase; it was one of the hottest cars that year. American Motors introduced completely redesigned Rambler Classic and Ambassador models for 1963. Doubtless these stole sales from Lark.

One of the most appealing 1963 Larks was this sharp Daytona hardtop with optional Skytop sunroof. These models are hard to find today and very desirable.

Perhaps the central reason for the decline was that Studebaker had simply failed to build sufficient momentum to keep moving forward. From 1961 to 1963, the company at times resembled a cold, tired engine trying to start. Mechanics know what that's like. Bang! A cylinder fires. Then nothing, then another bang, and another, then some hard cranking, a few more bangs, and for a few moments everything hangs in the balance, the engine seemingly ready to spring to life and run smoothly. Then a pop, bang, and a misfire, and the engine suddenly stops; and it's all over. For a while, the company seemed as if it would finally begin running strongly. But then came the misfires:

the strike, continued financial losses, the Avanti fiasco, quality problems, and before long, the engine died. For all its heroic efforts, Studebaker was simply unable to spark a recovery.

The results of the 1963 sales debacle showed up in the annual report. Most divisions reported increased sales, and total volume was $403 million, up a solid $38 million from the prior year. However, the company recorded an operating loss of $16.9 million for the year. The fault was almost entirely with the automotive division. Although Studebaker's acquired divisions had combined earnings of more than $11 million, the auto division lost more than $25 million. Clearly, the

The 1963 Lark Cruiser was the fanciest four-door Lark sedan that year and offered a plush interior. Inset in this photo is a shot of Brooks Stevens' clever in-dash vanity.

Studebaker issued this postcard showing the 1963 Lark Cruiser. Notice in the foreground the child's toy wagon, a replica of an 1800s Studebaker farm wagon in authentic colors.

This Lark Regal two-door sedan sold for $2,055. From the outside it's distinguishable from the Standard Lark by its full-length side molding and extra brightwork around the windows. A comparable Standard Lark listed for $1,935.

corporation couldn't long endure such losses; the situation called for drastic changes.

During the year, Egbert had championed an automotive program based upon a line of innovative new cars called the Avanti II. Originally planned to debut in 1964, these two- and four-door sedans were based on the existing Lark chassis but featured completely new styling created by Loewy. The Avanti II sedans were inspired by the Avanti coupe and were quite attractive. A Parisian coachbuilder produced full-size concept models, and if the cars had gone into production they would have been slotted above the Lark, with Studebaker evolving into a builder of premium automobiles aimed at enthusiasts desiring a well-styled performance car. Although Egbert made no public pronouncements about the Avanti II, it appears he hoped Studebaker would find a profitable niche marketing higher-margin automobiles.

As an alternative, Egbert also commissioned Brooks Stevens to create a line of more conventional cars. They represented the next generation of Larks but featured maximum interchangeability of body panels. The doors were cross-interchangeable, left rear identical to right front, to reduce tooling costs to a minimum. Stevens claimed his innovative design used many of the old Lark's inner panels.

Alas, only months after joining Studebaker, Egbert discovered he had cancer. In the ensuing time he'd had two surgeries, and by the end of 1963, he was tired and worn. With losses mounting, the board openly discussed liquidating the company, or at least its auto division. Egbert continued to argue in favor of the auto business, but in November 1963, as he faced another operation, the board put him on indefinite leave, appointing Finance Vice President Byers Burlingame to take his place.

Studebaker's unique sliding roof Wagonaire was useful in many ways. Here a flock of them are used as camera platforms. Other uses were for carrying tall items like plants and trees, surfboards, and so on. GM copied the sliding roof idea in the 1990s.

Egbert developed a plan to introduce a new line of Avanti-themed sedans and wagons built on the Lark chassis. They would have been introduced as a higher-priced series, then eventually would replace the Lark. *Photo courtesy John Hull*

There were two versions of the Avanti sedans produced for evaluation, the gold car with sharply peaked fenders and glitzy front-end brightwork and this black car with softer lines and less brightwork. *Photo courtesy John Hull*

A horse is a horse of course of course! Studebaker sponsored the hit TV program *Mister Ed* from 1961 to 1963. It starred Alan Young and Connie Hines, along with Mister Ed, a talking horse.

The fabulous Avanti for 1963, shown here at a dealer presentation. Notice the two-tone shoes worn by the man in the center and the bags of balloons hanging overhead. It's difficult to understand why a car as exciting as the Avanti didn't sell better.

The beautiful 1964 Gran Turismo Hawk was one of the best-looking cars on the road. The GT Hawk was fairly unique among U.S. cars, being one of the few four-passenger sport coupes. *Photo courtesy Mike Mueller*

Completely new front-end styling marked the new Studebaker Larks for 1964. The naming got a little confusing, since the company called the base series Lark Challenger and the up-level models the Lark Commander. The gold car in the foreground is a Commander four-door sedan. The white four-door and blue two-door are Challengers. The Challenger series was dropped with the closing of South Bend, so all were built in late 1963.

Studebaker had reached another crossroads. The auto division's huge losses strapped corporate finances. The company had borrowed $25 million for the Franklin purchase but got the banks to agree to stretch out the payments. However, the banks refused to lend any more money for the auto division unless the corporation agreed to put up its acquired divisions as collateral. That was something the board was unwilling to do. To put the company's profitable divisions in jeopardy for the sake of the auto division was too risky. Their fiduciary responsibilities were clear; they must protect the stockholders' investment.

This left the automotive division on a short string. From that point on, it would have to pay its own way. Lacking the ability to borrow

money to produce either the Avanti II or Stevens' new Larks, all that could be done was another facelift of a now-ancient body. The company managed to restyle the Lark once more, giving it a nearly all-new appearance for 1964. If these models sold well the division might be able to continue on. If not . . .

Introduced in late September, the 1964 Larks were one of Brooks Stevens' greater accomplishments. Front sheet metal was completely new, with appealing angular styling. A modern, full-width grille that made the car appear much wider replaced the Mercedes-style grille, while the crisp new roofline was reminiscent of the GT Hawk. Many considered the 1964 the best-looking Lark of all. Only the rear fenders

Since the truck line was dropped with the closure of the South Bend operations, all 1964 Studebaker trucks were produced during the final months of 1963. It was a shame; Studebaker had pioneered light-duty diesel trucks, which today are a huge market.

betrayed it wasn't an all-new car. Three series were offered in six-cylinder and V-8 models: the Challenger, Commander, and Daytona. A high-trim V-8 Cruiser was also included. Both the Gran Turismo Hawk and the Avanti returned with minor updating.

Initially, it looked as if things might turn around. October 1963 sales were up more than 10 percent over October 1962. But in November, sales resumed their downward slide. With an 86-day supply of new cars in dealer's hands and 3,000 1963 models still unshipped, production was halted for a week to reduce inventory levels. The company was drowning in red ink.

By early December, the mounting losses could no longer be endured. The board of directors made a last-ditch effort to find a solution, but none could be found. On December 7 the decision was made: Studebaker's South Bend plant would be shut down permanently. Car production would continue on a greatly reduced scale at the company's plant in Hamilton, Ontario, Canada.

When the news was announced on December 9 it shot through South Bend like lightning. Although everyone knew the company was in trouble, the idea that after 111 years Studebaker would close the factory and leave town was simply unthinkable. One worker refused to believe it at first, angrily calling it "another dirty management trick to scare us." Another heatedly told a TV news reporter that "Studebaker will still be here when you're dead and gone!" Eleven days later, the line shut down for good.

The 1964 Avanti's square headlight frames are generally considered a mark of the 1964 models, but that's only a guideline. It was a running change, and some 1964s have the round headlamp frames.

As Burlingame and board chairman Randolph Guthrie explained it, "The basic difficulty in South Bend was insufficient volume of sales. Our facilities there were such that there was no way to reduce our costs so that a profit could be made upon such volume. The Canadian plant on the other hand is relatively modern and it can be operated at a profit on much lower volume. Therefore we have decided to live with the sales we have rather than to continue to hope they will improve." With noticeable relief, they stated that "Studebaker has now moved into a new period in its corporate history. It is now a diversified company of which only one of its many activities is the manufacture of automobiles." They stated that Franklin's sales volume might exceed automotive sales in the coming year.

Closing South Bend would be expensive. The company took a special charge of $64 million to cover anticipated losses on disposal of the plant, property, equipment, and tools, along with inventory write-downs. Adding the special charge to the operating deficit brought the total loss for 1963 to an unbelievable $80.9 million. The company's cash fell to just $8.3 million; retained earnings went from a positive $43 million to a negative $37.8 million. At year end, the company's net worth was a mere $36.7 million.

(Above) Since it was a commercial failure, the company decided to discontinue the Avanti when it closed out its South Bend auto and truck assembly plants. Thus, like the truck models, all 1964 Avantis were produced in South Bend during 1963.

(Left) The 1964 Lark Commander offered great new styling but failed to sell in expected volume. By December 1963, Studebaker's Automotive Division was forced to cease U.S. production of cars and trucks.

The last year Studebaker would offer convertibles was 1964. This lovely Lark soft-top shows how beautifully Brooks Stevens was able to update the Lark styling on a minimal budget.

Beginning January 1964, Studebaker's Canadian plant became the sole source of cars for the United States and Canada. It was a great deal smaller than South Bend, but with a few improvements could produce upward of 36,000 cars annually. Break-even had been in the range of 7,000 to 8,000 cars; but once South Bend closed down, the Hamilton operation had to bear the entire sales division overhead. The break-even point rose sharply to more than 20,000 units. To maximize efficiency, all Hawk and truck models were dropped. The Avanti had flopped, so it,

too, was dropped from the line. The low-buck Challenger series was deleted so production could concentrate on the more profitable Commander, Daytona, and Cruiser models.

Once Studebaker announced the transfer of auto production to Canada, retail sales in the United States collapsed. Total car sales in the United States and Canada fell sharply to just 35,373 from 73,277 the prior year. However, since Hamilton had produced only 17,438 cars by year end, the majority of cars sold during 1964 were units

(Above) Jane Kmita, still listed as Miss Dominion of Canada, is pictured with her new Studebaker Daytona convertible. During this year all Studebaker car production was transferred to the Canadian plant in Hamilton, Ontario.

(Left) This is a 1964 advertisement for Gravely tractors. By 1964 Studebaker had acquired enough other businesses that it could survive without the auto division. Since it was losing so much money on cars, the company decided to downsize its operations by moving all auto production into a small plant in Canada.

Because of the upheaval caused by closing down South Bend operations, there weren't a lot of visual changes to the 1965 Studebakers. But under the hood there now resided GM engines, produced in Canada.

produced in South Bend before the end of 1963. The company anticipated a further sales drop for 1965.

Other parts of Studebaker Corporation had problems, too. Domowatt ended up being a mistake, running into financial problems almost immediately after its purchase. During the year, Domowatt, which had been folded into Franklin Appliance earlier, disappeared from the corporate statements. Even the plant in Italy was no longer listed under Franklin assets. Trans International Airlines had rung up substantial indebtedness for aircraft purchases.

When management reported to stockholders on the corporation's 1964 results, they stated that "problems still exist in establishing a profitable basis for the Corporation's automotive operations," adding that the break-even point was being reduced to approximately 20,000 units. The company was also exploring the possibility of importing a low-priced foreign car for its dealers to sell. They already had Mercedes-Benz, which was very successful, and DKW–Auto Union, which was a complete flop. Earlier they'd investigated and rejected the Goggomobil, a little German economy

The 1965 Studebaker model lineup was trimmed down considerably from the prior year. The handsome Cruiser was offered in six- and eight-cylinder versions.

bug that was an even worse tin can than the DKW. Now their attentions turned to Japan and the possibility of importing Toyota, a virtually unknown brand.

The effect of the South Bend closeout was immediately apparent in the financial results. Total volume fell to $261 million, a drop of more than $140 million! Yet amazingly, the company recorded a profit of $8 million, which was tax-free. It was the first significant profit since 1959.

Equally as important was what had been accomplished in reducing corporate debt. At the beginning of 1964, total debt stood at more than

$56 million. But during the year, the company sold automotive properties, including a foundry, body plant, engine plant, assembly plant, stamping plant, power house, and other buildings, for a total of $13 million, which was applied to debt reduction. Trans International Airlines, burdened with debt, was also sold.

The military truck plant was sold to Kaiser Jeep Corporation and the contract transferred to them. The move greatly helped Kaiser, giving it larger, more expensive military products to supplement sales of military Jeeps. One might ponder at this point how differently things might

One of the casualties of the move to Canada was the hardtop body style, so the two-door 1965 Daytona was a sport sedan rather than a hardtop. The Daytona convertible and four-door sedans were also gone, but a Daytona wagon remained in the lineup.

have turned out if Studebaker management had bought Kaiser Jeep (née Willys Motors) as one of its acquisitions. Kaiser Industries was interested in selling, and if Studebaker had bought or merged with Jeep, there's a good chance they would have survived as an automaker. In any event, many Studebaker workers ended up employed by Kaiser Jeep in the Chippewa Avenue plant, building heavy-duty trucks for the armed forces.

The auto division was still in trouble. Hamilton's break-even was 20,000 units against the 17,438 cars produced during 1964, so

production had to increase, meaning the company needed its dealers to order (and sell) more than 20,000 cars in 1965. During 1964, the 325 Canadian dealers had retailed 7,658 cars while 1,700 U.S. dealers sold 27,715, so retailing more than 20,000 cars for 1965 wasn't an unreasonable target.

Once South Bend stopped producing engines, the company had to source them from another party. McKinnon Industries of St. Catherine's, Ontario, a GM subsidiary, signed on to supply Chevrolet engines for the 1965s. (One can't help but wonder if

THE COMMON-SENSE CAR

Production of the new 1965 Studebaker cars began in August 1964, with introduction scheduled for October. There were no styling changes—the company called this its policy of continuity of styling—but they announced that Studebaker would offer the largest list of standard equipment in its price class. Standard equipment included a dual master cylinder, finned brake drums, quad headlamps, dual horns, dual sun visors, two-speed electric wipers, windshield wipers, alternator, cigar lighter, padded instrument panel, inside hood lock, and much more.

Hamilton's work force was increased from 700 to 1,100 people. A greatly slimmed-down 1965 lineup included ten models: Commander two- and four-door sedans plus a wagon and a Cruiser four-door, all with either six-cylinder or V-8 engines. The Daytona V-8 line offered a Sport two-door sedan and a four-door wagon. The six-cylinder Daytonas were no longer offered. The gorgeous

AMC had been approached, though probably it wasn't.) The Chevy 194-cid six may have been uninspired, but it was reliable and smooth. Chevrolet's 283 V-8, on the other hand, was one of the best V-8s ever built.

The Daytona, too, was an attractive sporty compact despite not offering hardtop or convertible models. But one has to wonder how much better Studebaker might have done in 1965 with a full range of Daytona body styles.

With the Challengers gone, the volume sellers in the Studebaker line were the attractive and well-priced Commanders. Studebaker claimed its cars offered more standard equipment than other cars in its class.

convertibles and hardtops were also gone, as was the Commander Special two-door sedan introduced in 1964. There were no taxi, fleet, or police models listed either. These product moves were curiously shortsighted for a company supposedly trying to sell as many cars as possible.

In any event, only 19,435 Studebakers were produced for the 1965 model year. Sources state that production during the calendar year was 18,542 (though that excludes '65s built in the final quarter of 1964 and includes 1966 cars built in late 1965). While both numbers were slightly below the stated break-even point, one can only guess how many more cars would have been built if convertibles and hardtops had been produced, if the low-priced Challengers hadn't been dropped, if Taxi and Police models were marketed strongly, or even if the Hawk was still being built.

Gordon Grundy, president of Studebaker's auto division, found an innovative way to offset some of its cost. New trade rules allowed home market producers to import cars into Canada duty-free. Grundy made a deal with Volkswagen. Since the average duty on a VW was $165, Grundy offered to act as importer, buying VWs in Germany, selling them to Volkswagen Canada for $15 less

The good-looking 1965 Studebaker Commander four-door sedan was an economical and attractive family car.

than they had been paying, and retaining the $150 per car difference as profit. It was entirely a paper transaction, and both parties benefited.

Grundy also made a proposal to Nissan that Studebaker become North American distributor for their cars and trucks. Reportedly, the two firms were nearing an agreement when Grundy was told to break off the talks and approach Toyota instead. The gambit didn't work; Toyota didn't like being second choice, and Nissan refused to reopen talks after being shunted aside. According to sources, the switch had come about after Randolph Guthrie mentioned the impending deal to a partner in his law firm, Richard M.

Nixon. Apparently it was in Nixon's interest that Toyota be approached instead, and he urged Guthrie to order Grundy to pull back from the Nissan talks. True or not, the Nissan and Toyota deals were both dead.

For 1965, Studebaker Corporation reported a total sales volume of $192 million, a drop of $69 million from the prior year. Income, however, rose to $10.7 million, a 32 percent increase. Corporate debt was reduced to just $13 million. Over two years the company had eliminated $43 million of its debt. It's important to note that the company still had $30 million in tax-loss carry-forward credits, most of which would be available through 1969.

The 1966 Studebakers were introduced in September 1965, wearing attractive new styling created by independent design firm Marcks, Hazelquist and Powers of Dearborn, Michigan. They were quite good-looking, and it's a shame the line didn't sell better. This is the Daytona Sports Sedan, available with a choice of six- or eight-cylinder engine.

During 1965 the company formed a new division: StudeGrip, engaged in the manufacture and sale of metal tire studs. The company had acquired the rights to manufacture a Finnish company's patented design. During the year, Studebaker became the largest supplier of studs in the industry.

There were signs management's heart wasn't in the auto business. In February 1965, the company sold the assets and North American distribution rights for Mercedes-Benz to Daimler-Benz.

The corporation then applied about $9 million of the sales price to debt reduction. But selling Mercedes-Benz meant the loss of one of the automotive division's profit-makers.

Details of the 1966 models were released in May 1965, rather early but probably done to reassure the public that the company would continue in business. Since the styling department had been phased out after South Bend's closure, Grundy had to hire outside designers to give

Studebaker's new grille for 1966 was pleasingly simple, with a certain elegance of design. It somehow made the entire car look new. Imagine how much better the cars might have sold if this design had debuted on the 1965 models.

the cars a facelift. He settled on an outstanding firm: Marcks, Hazelquist and Powers of Dearborn, Michigan. Bob Marcks was a car designer extraordinaire, an ex-Loewy designer who was able to give the aging Studebaker a fresh new look.

The 1966 Studebakers were quite attractive. What Marcks, Hazelquist and Powers accomplished on a miniscule budget was extraordinary. A stylish new grille comprising four rectangular

floating sections linked at the center with a new emblem gave a fresh new appearance up front. Two multi-beam lamps replaced the quad headlamps.

Bodyside bright trim was placed lower where it could double as a rub rail while giving the car a lower appearance. Out back, the area above the taillamp housings included ventilation louvers for the new "Refreshaire" ventilating system, in which outside air was introduced

Appearing for the last time was the Cruiser. It was a sad passing for a great car.

through cowl vents and stale, smoky air expelled through the rear vent ports. Grundy said the changes for 1966 were dictated by practicality, usefulness, and durability.

Bob Marcks wanted to significantly upgrade the car's image, so he chose rich fabrics and elegant colors of the sort one usually saw in Cadillacs. The difference in look and feel was substantial. Six new metallic exterior colors included Niagara Blue Mist, Timberline Turquoise, Yellowknife Gold, Mount Royal Red (offered only through December 1965), Algonquin Green, and Richelieu Blue. All had

distinctly Canadian-sounding names. Adding to the rich look was wood-grain material applied to instrument panels on all models and on Daytona and Cruiser door panels. New safety equipment included padded sun visors and no-glare wiper arms.

Introduction was set for late September. The lineup included Commander two- and four-door sedans, a Wagonaire, a Daytona two-door sedan, and a Cruiser four-door, all with a choice of six or V-8 power. Prices began as low as $2,060. The company also announced it would "continue to build a single taxicab model as a

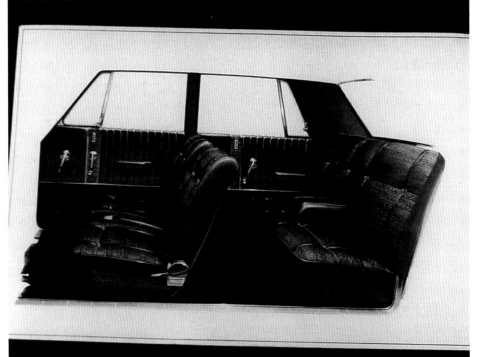

Designer Bob Marcks created posh new interior designs for Studebaker, and the company said the new interiors were the most stylish in Studebaker history.

special order, rugged duty vehicle, available to any buyer." This was curious, since they hadn't mentioned it during the 1965 announcement. In December 1965, the factory added Highlander Red and Plum to the exterior color choices.

Marcks, Hazelquist and Powers prepared a prototype 1967 model and began work on future models, but when Grundy asked the board for funding for the new 1967 cars he was told there would be no 1967 models. On March 4, the corporation announced that car production was ending the following day. Only 2,045 cars had been produced during calendar year 1966, an annual rate equal to 12,000 units per year.

And there lies a problem, because Gordon Grundy always claimed that his division was operating profitably at the time of the closure. However, when they announced the final end, management blamed it on "heavy and irreversible losses" in the auto division. There's been some speculation, however, that what really happened was the corporation had either become embarrassed by the auto division (unlikely) or had lost interest in it, depending on who's talking. Others have stated that the heavy losses were really only lost opportunities, actual lost potential income rather than lost profits. But the company statement said neither. It spoke clearly of

Styling details of the 1966 models are shown clockwise from the upper right: the new grille theme, the "Refreshaire" rear vents, the instrument panel and wheel, and the Daytona's sharp interior.

"heavy and irreversible losses." So either Grundy or the company was wrong.

There are several possible explanations. It may be that when Grundy said his division was operating profitably, he meant it had for 1965. That's possible, since production came close to the break-even point. Or perhaps Grundy was including the substantial income the division received acting as the middleman for VW of Canada, income that would end when the rules changed. Or perhaps his memory was faulty. Certainly that has happened enough times in history.

The facts tend to support management's statement. After all, the break-even point was something over 20,000 cars in 1964 and hadn't been reached. Even after it was reduced to 20,000 units (which works out to only about 10 cars per year for each of Studebaker's 2,000 U.S. and Canadian dealers), Hamilton failed to reach it. An auto company,

From the upper right are the Daytona sports sedan, Wagonaire, Commander two- and four-door sedans, and Cruiser. Studebaker was a fine old company, and its passing left a great many sad. The Studebaker Drivers Club, the largest independent car club in America, celebrates the great Studebaker heritage.

or any company for that matter, cannot operate for long at break-even. Sooner or later a profit must be made. This is especially true in the automobile business because its size and scale means that when losses occur they tend to be catastrophic. Over the years Studebaker had withstood as many catastrophic losses as it could handle. The board wanted to see no more.

And so the journey that began in Indiana ended in Canada. The great old Studebaker Corporation, heir to greatness and home to so many memories, left the transportation industry. Although it was sad to lose so great an automaker, many other companies had gone before it, vanishing without a trace. Studebaker left behind a heritage of great cars and trucks, and that rich legacy is something that will never fade away.

The design firm of Marcks, Hazelquist and Powers was hired to create styling changes on the 1966 Studebaker line. Once that was completed, the designers began work on the 1967 Studebaker, seen here in front of the offices of Marcks, Hazelquist and Powers.

CHAPTER EIGHT

1967–1970
Studebaker Is Dead;
Long Live Studebaker!

Weeks before Studebaker announced it was leaving the automobile business, the firm of Marcks, Hazelquist and Powers (MHP) had nearly completed designing the 1967 models. Designer Bob Marcks was able to greatly improve the Studebaker's appearance with only minor changes. "One of the problems with the 1964–66 Studebakers," he recalled, "was that they had a very high-looking back end. One day I noticed a Mustang and Studebaker parked side by side in a lot. The Mustang's higher bumpers helped make it look low." He felt the Studebaker's low-set bumper in comparison made the car look dumpy.

So MHP mocked up a 1967 concept using a 1966 model as the base car. Marcks raised the rear bumper to just below the decklid, greatly improving the appearance. He kept the 1967 grille design simple, two panels inside a larger rectangle. Using pieces of simple colored cardboard, the designer also mocked up new rear styling with faired-in rear fenders. Wide bodyside moldings similar to the 1964–'65 style were added, placed beneath the door handles for a lower look. The 1967 Studebaker's styling was a handsome update and compared well with others in its market segment.

Inspired, Marcks began to create proposals for possible designs to carry Studebaker to 1968, 1969, 1970, and beyond. Realizing a

The car on the left is a production 1966 Studebaker. On the right is a prototype of a 1967 model. Notice how the higher rear bumper gives the 1967 model a sleeker and more modern look. In this photo the side trim is above the door handle line.

Marcks, Hazelquist and Powers explored many ideas for 1967 and beyond. Judging by the exterior trim details, this handsome sedan appears to be a 1967 Cruiser, or perhaps a 1968.

A simplified yet stylish new grille was the focal point of the 1967's front-end theme. Notice the wide body molding running below the door handle line.

Another future Studebaker, this circa 1967–1969 mock-up has interesting trim. Notice how the bright work runs along the top of both doors, then moves upward to meet the vinyl top moldings.

Designer Bob Marcks was determined to upgrade the cars' image via extra-stylish interiors.

complete redesign was out of the question, MHP focused on a major restyling of the existing car. One was a four-door sedan with Hawk styling themes; another featured a sloping hood and twin grille openings like the legendary 1953 models. All design work was done between December 1965 and February 1966, and all the proposals were modifications of the existing four-door sedan using the same wheelbase, cowl, windshield, and doors.

Two interesting concepts brought the Studebaker line to 1970. The deep maroon car shown in the accompanying photograph might be considered a Studebaker Cruiser for later in the decade. Marcks felt the existing tooling could be modified to create a six-window greenhouse.

A gold four-door sedan represented what a midsize Studebaker might have looked like in 1970. Marcks recalled: "The basic body shell

was retained but with modified rear door upper frames and new rear quarters. The front end had Avanti-style blade fenders and a '53-style rear deck. We thought there was a possibility of finding the Hawk grille tooling for the Hawk-like front end."

The concepts illustrate how Studebaker might have continued into the 1970s, offering a modern car with distinctive styling. Certainly these cars would have appealed to Studebaker's traditional customers, and if looks sell cars, the MHP proposals probably would have brought in many conquest sales as well. Who can say how long the automobile line might have lasted? When it was all over for the car division, E. J. Challinor, president of Studebaker Automotive Sales Corporation in South Bend, sent Marcks a letter stating that "my entire organization [has] only the highest regard for you and your people and we . . . will miss not having the opportunity to work with

Using the Hawk theme as his inspiration, Marcks designed this gorgeous four-door sedan with blade-type front fenders, Hawk hood and grille, and a squared-off roofline. The car is based on the Lark Daytona/Commander shell and could have been produced for a relatively modest investment. It's a pity this design wasn't around in 1962 as a companion to the Gran Turismo Hawk coupe.

Marcks believed this attractive car could be produced using the same basic body as before but with minor retooling of the "C" pillar and roof panel, along with new fenders. Notice how luxurious this car looks.

Another Marcks idea was this coupe, again using the existing body. The padded roof helps to disguise its Lark heritage. American Motors used a similar approach in 1978 when it created the Concord D/L from the old Hornet sedan.

This stunning beauty is a proposal for a 1970 or later Studebaker sedan. Bob Marcks believed that moving the Studebaker line upscale would improve its image and profitability. This would have been a very exciting car had it been produced.

Brooks Stevens also had some ideas for future Studebaker cars. This sharp two-door hardtop is the Sceptre, an idea for a GT Hawk–type sport coupe.

you . . . in development of new car designs which I feel certain would have been successful."

Brooks Stevens had also worked out ideas for future Studebaker cars. His 1966 Sceptre proposal was a concept of what a future Hawk-type car might look like. Very low and sleek, it managed to retain the GT Hawk's flavor in a totally new package. Alas, by the time the Sceptre was ready, the fate of the auto division had already been decided.

Naturally, the business of the corporation continued on after the car division shut down. Indeed, the whole point of closing out auto production was to save what was left of the company and use it as a

foundation to grow on. A new acquisition was Big Four Industries, principal U.S. maker of tire studding guns and also a maker of tire changers. StudeGrip operations were merged into the Big Four.

When the company reported business results for 1966, it appeared that sales volume had dropped again, to $172 million. However, management for some reason had chosen to exclude automotive sales from the 1966 numbers. Only a small note at the bottom of a page revealed that automotive sales weren't included. It provided a breakout of automotive sales for 1965 (they'd been just under $45 million) but provided no comparable figure for 1966. Why management chose not to report on the auto division for 1966 is a puzzle.

As a concept car, the Sceptre was treated to some unusual features of the type that show cars often have. One such feature was this light-bar. Created by Sylvania, it replaced the conventional headlamps and was said to provide better light.

Sceptre also had this pop-up vanity, similar in theme to the earlier one Stevens had designed for production Studebakers.

New GRAVELY Convertible Tractor
makes tough jobs easy...simple jobs a pleasure!

Here's the power partner you've always wanted . . . the Gravely Convertible that gives you the best *of both worlds*. Now you sit back and ride through those big lawn areas . . . in command all the way. Your all-gear, no-belt drive gives you instant control, and that new Gravely engine gives you power to spare. Four speeds forward, four reverse . . . without clutching. Safe, comfortable, almost indestructible!

When the going gets rough... pull one pin and your rider converts to a walker. Takes to steep terrain like a mountain goat . . . does the tough trimming, the gardening and rugged clearing jobs with ease.

Four-season performance... with your choice from 39 attachments that give you power to mow, plow, blow snow, haul or do any other lawn and garden job — better! For as low as $27.07 a month*, you can own the new Gravely Convertible with 40" mower! See your Gravely dealer for exact price in your area. Send for our FREE CATALOG. Write now: Gravely, 5604 Gravely Lane, Dunbar, W. Va. 25064.

After minimum down payment

◈ GRAVELY TRACTOR DIVISION **Studebaker** CORPORATION

COMMERCIAL-10 SUPER L CONVERTIBLE

The newest in compact tractors from the oldest compact tractor manufacturer—1917-1967

Walking Versatility

Riding Convenience

with Wagner Electric Corporation about a possible merger.

During the confusing corporate situation in 1966, management decided to shed some losers the company had picked up along the way. Cincinnati Testing Laboratories, with annual sales of less than $2 million, was sold during 1966. Franklin Appliance, which by then was barely profitable, was sold to White Consolidated Industries. Studebaker's best-performing divisions were Clarke Floor Machines, Gravely Tractors (they were later joined to form Clarke-Gravely Division), Schaefer, Chemical Compounds (which eventually was renamed STP Corporation), and Onan. All five continued to grow and were solidly profitable.

In 1967, Studebaker, Wagner Electric, and Worthington Industries came together to form Studebaker-Worthington Inc. With Studebaker's profitable divisions, Wagner Electric's automotive electrical and brake businesses, and Worthington's diverse holdings— including construction equipment and valve

In any event, net income for 1966 rose sharply to $16.4 million. With strong profits and no automotive division to worry about, other companies became interested in Studebaker as a partner. The fact that some tax-loss carry-forwards remained available made it an even better prospect for merger. The company reported on talks held and power generation businesses—the corporation grew. Annual sales revenue for 1967 exceeded $650 million. Although there no longer were any significant operations in South Bend, there was still Studebaker flavor in the newly merged company. Randolph Guthrie was chairman, and Byers Burlingame served on the board of directors.

Unexcelled for Prestige...

Catch a fleeting glance of the aerodynamic Avanti II and you may have to catch your breath a second later. Truly, here is a breath-taking departure in automotive styling. From any angle, here is a truly, totally different automobile, yet its arresting style is based on practical aerodynamics. Fully equipped with every power assist, disc brakes, air conditioning, radio, heater, premium white wall tires, customized decorator interior fabrics and dozens of other deluxe features, the new Avanti II is sheer sophistication in motion. But, moving or standing still, this motor car spells "prestige" in big, bold capital letters.

Unlimited choice of luxurious, decorator fabric, materials and patterns are available to complement the Avanti II's handsome interior styling. Extra features like beauty vanity (at right) are apparent throughout.

Former Studebaker dealer Nate Altman bought the rights and tooling for the Avanti and reintroduced it in 1966 as a hand-built prestige car. The company was successful for many years.

During 1969, Andy Granatelli's "STP Oil Treatment Special" racecar won the Indianapolis 500 with Mario Andretti at the wheel. The following year Byers Burlingame, the man who had authorized closing South Bend, passed away. In 1973, the tenth anniversary of South Bend's closing, Studebaker-Worthington sales exceeded $1 billion for the first time. By that point, Onan sales alone were more than $100 million, STP sales were $87 million, Clarke-Gravely sales were $58 million, and Schaeffer sales just under $10 million. This shows that if Studebaker had remained independent rather than merging it still would have had sales of well over $250 million per year.

As corporations go, Studebaker-Worthington didn't last very long. Its last full year was 1978; after that it was acquired by McGraw-Edison. A few years after that, McGraw-Edison was absorbed by Cooper Industries. With no attachment to any product then in production, the Studebaker name itself faded.

Brooks Stevens created a retro-styled Studebaker-powered roadster for the New York Auto Show. Called the Studebaker SS, it evolved into a hand-built specialty car called the Excalibur.

Long before that, however, the heart had gone out of the company. Reading through the annual reports of Studebaker-Worthington, one is struck by the almost complete lack of any expression of pride in being a manufacturer, a builder of things. The company rarely boasted about its products; how fine they worked or how well they were made. There were no slogans to stir one's blood, no "Owe No Man Anything but to Love One Another" or "Always Give the Customer More Than You Promise." Instead, there were boasts about how much money was being made and how much greater the profit margin had grown. The company had become a gray, joyless corporation, without passion and without soul. J. M., old "Wheelbarrow Johnny," would have wept.

In that regard, Studebaker was dead. But in a more important sense, Studebaker lives and breathes. It remains hale and hearty. Like a vast oak tree, Studebaker spread its seeds, and some of them burst forth in bloom. Brooks Stevens' sons created the Excalibur automobile from a special show car their father had built called the Studebaker SS. A retro-styled beauty, it remained in production for more than 20 years.

Studebaker dealer Nate Altman purchased the rights and tooling for the Avanti, and the brand has continued, with some bumps along the way, to the present. Another offshoot, the Studebaker-Worthington Leasing Corporation, which came into being around 1972, remains in business, having survived the ever-changing corporate shakeups.

But of far greater importance than any of those firms is the Studebaker Drivers Club, home to many thousands of enthusiastic fans of South Bend's greatest company. They've remained loyal to the Studebaker name and have stood by Studebaker through good times and bad. The passion and faithfulness shown by club members ensure that Studebaker will live for all time.

From the ashes of Studebaker's automotive empire sprang forth a few small firms that built cars. Excalibur was the first of the retro-styled cars and probably the most successful, producing the popular cars for more than two decades.

189

Index